# Diabetic LIVING®
# Everyday
## COOKING VOLUME 11

DIABETIC LIVING® EVERYDAY COOKING
IS PART OF A BOOK SERIES
PUBLISHED BY BETTER HOMES AND
GARDENS SPECIAL INTEREST·MEDIA,
DES MOINES, IOWA

# Diabetic LIVING Everyday COOKING VOLUME 11

## CONSUMER MARKETING

| | |
|---|---|
| Vice President, Consumer Marketing | STEVE CROWE |
| Director of Direct Marketing–Books | DANIEL FAGAN |
| Marketing Operations Manager | MAX DAILY |
| Assistant Marketing Manager | KYLIE DAZZO |
| Production Manager | LIZ WARD |
| Contributing Project Manager | SHELLI MCCONNELL, PURPLE PEAR PUBLISHING, INC. |
| Contributing Art Director | SHELLEY CALDWELL |
| Contributing Food Stylist | LAUREN MCANELLY |
| Photographer | BRIE PASSANO |
| Test Kitchen Director | LYNN BLANCHARD |

## DIABETIC LIVING® MAGAZINE

| | |
|---|---|
| Editorial Director | JESSIE PRICE |
| Executive Editor | LAUREN LASTOWKA |
| Creative Director | JAMES VAN FLETEREN |
| Associate Editor | MICAELA YOUNG, M.S. |
| Managing Editor | WENDY S. RUOPP, M.S. |

## MEREDITH NATIONAL MEDIA GROUP

President, Consumer Products  TOM WITSCHI

President and Chief Executive Officer  TOM HARTY

Vice Chairman  MELL MEREDITH FRAZIER

*Diabetic Living® Everyday Cooking* is part of a series published by Meredith Corp., 1716 Locust St., Des Moines, IA 50309-3023.

If you have comments or questions about the editorial material in *Diabetic Living® Everyday Cooking*, write to the editor of *Diabetic Living*, Meredith Corp., 1716 Locust St., Des Moines, IA 50309-3023. Send an email to *DiabeticLiving.Specials.com*

*Diabetic Living®* magazine is available by subscription or on the newsstand. To order a subscription to the magazine, go to *dlvcustserv@cdsfullfillment.com*

# CONTENTS

Springtime
Cacio e Pepe,
p. 30

# 1
# FAMILY-PLEASING
# DINNERS

Turn boring dinnertime into a delicious, health-smart opportunity. Build your meal around these nutritious options, each created with the right balance of carbs, protein, and fat. Many of these good-for-all recipes include directions for two meals—bake one now, freeze one for later.

### Chicken and Veggie Fajitas

**35g**
**CARB**

SERVES 4
TOTAL 25 min.

2 tsp. canola or olive oil
1 lb. skinless, boneless chicken thighs, trimmed and cut into strips
4 cups thinly sliced vegetables, such as onions, bell peppers, zucchini, and/or mushrooms
1¼ tsp. chili powder
¼ tsp. salt
4 8-inch whole wheat tortillas
½ cup guacamole
½ cup plain fat-free Greek yogurt
1 lime, cut into wedges
¼ cup fresh cilantro leaves (optional)

**1.** In a large wok or cast-iron skillet heat oil over high. Add chicken, vegetables, chili powder, and salt; cook about 7 minutes or until chicken is cooked through and vegetables begin to brown, tossing with tongs occasionally.

**2.** Meanwhile, stack tortillas and wrap in a barely damp clean kitchen towel (or paper towel). Microwave 30 to 45 seconds.

**3.** Divide the chicken-and-vegetable mixture among the tortillas. Top with guacamole and yogurt. Serve with lime wedges and, if desired, garnish with cilantro.

**PER SERVING** (1 fajita each) **CAL** 391, **FAT** 13 g (2 g sat. fat), **CHOL** 92 mg, **SODIUM** 699 mg, **CARB** 35 g (6 g fiber, 7 g sugars), **PRO** 32 g

## Chicken-Spaghetti Squash Bake

**19g CARB**

SERVES 8
HANDS ON 55 min.
TOTAL 1 hr. 40 min.

- 1 medium spaghetti squash (about 3 lb.)
- 4 cups broccoli florets
- 1 Tbsp. canola oil
- 1 10-oz. pkg. sliced fresh mushrooms
- 1 medium onion, finely chopped
- 2 cloves garlic, minced
- ½ tsp. dried thyme
- ½ tsp. black pepper
- 2 10-oz. cans reduced-sodium condensed cream of mushroom soup, such as Campbell's 25% Less Sodium
- 1½ lb. skinless, boneless chicken breasts, cut into bite-size pieces
- ½ cup shredded extra-sharp cheddar cheese

**1.** Preheat oven to 375°F. Coat two 8-inch square baking dishes with *nonstick cooking spray*.

**2.** Halve squash lengthwise and scoop out the seeds. Place halves, cut sides down, in a microwave-safe dish; add 2 Tbsp. water. Microwave, uncovered, 10 to 12 minutes or until the flesh can be scraped with a fork but is still crisp-tender. Scrape the flesh into strands onto a plate.

**3.** Place broccoli in the same dish; add 1 Tbsp. water and cover. Microwave 2 to 3 minutes or until just barely crisp-tender, stirring occasionally. Drain; set aside to cool.

**4.** Meanwhile, in a large nonstick skillet heat oil over medium-high. Add mushrooms; cook and stir about 8 minutes or until they've released their juices. Add onion and continue cooking about 8 minutes or until onion is tender and the mushrooms are lightly browned.

**5.** Stir in garlic, thyme, and pepper; cook and stir 30 seconds, Stir in soup (do not dilute with water); heat through. Stir in chicken, squash, and broccoli; gently toss to combine.

**6.** Divide the mixture between the prepared baking dishes. Sprinkle each with ¼ cup cheese. Cover with foil. Label and freeze one casserole up to 1 month.*

**7.** Bake the remaining casserole, covered, about 25 minutes or until bubbling. Uncover; continue baking 10 to 25 minutes or until lightly browned at edges. Let stand 10 minutes before serving.

**\*TIP** Thaw frozen casserole overnight in the refrigerator. If desired, spoon off any liquid that has accumulated in the pan. Bake as directed.

**PER SERVING** (one 4-inch square each)
**CAL** 273, **FAT** 11 g (3 g sat. fat), **CHOL** 71 mg,
**SODIUM** 493 mg, **CARB** 19 g (5 g fiber, 6 g sugars),
**PRO** 25 g

Grilled Chicken Breasts with Tomato-Caper Sauce

## Sheet-Pan Orange-Apricot Drumsticks

**41g CARB**

SERVES 4
HANDS ON 25 min.
TOTAL 1 hr.

- 1 lb. multicolor fingerling potatoes, halved lengthwise
- 1 lb. thin green beans, trimmed
- 1 cup halved and thinly sliced red onion
- 2 Tbsp. olive oil
- ¾ tsp. kosher salt
- ¼ tsp. black pepper
- 1 orange
- 3 Tbsp. apricot preserves
- 1 Tbsp. reduced-sodium soy sauce
- 3 cloves garlic, minced
  Dash black pepper
- 4 large chicken drumsticks (1½ to 2 lb. total), skinned

**1.** Preheat oven to 425°F. Place potatoes in a large microwave-safe bowl; cover. Microwave 2 minutes.
**2.** In a rimmed baking sheet combine potatoes, green beans, and onion. Drizzle with oil and sprinkle with ½ tsp. of the salt and the ¼ tsp. pepper.
**3.** For glaze, remove ½ tsp. zest and squeeze 2 Tbsp. juice from the orange. In a small bowl combine zest, juice, preserves, soy sauce, garlic, the dash pepper, and the remaining ¼ tsp. salt. Nestle chicken into vegetables and brush chicken with half of the glaze.
**4.** Roast 15 minutes. Remove from oven. Stir vegetables; turn chicken and brush with the remaining glaze. Roast about 20 minutes more or until chicken is done (at least 175°F) and potatoes are tender.

**PER SERVING** (1 drumstick + 1½ cups vegetables each) **CAL** 328, **FAT** 10 g (2 g sat. fat), **CHOL** 60 mg, **SODIUM** 432 mg, **CARB** 41 g (7 g fiber, 14 g sugars), **PRO** 20 g

## Grilled Chicken Breasts with Tomato-Caper Sauce

**6g CARB**

SERVES 4
TOTAL 30 min.

- 1½ tsp. olive oil
- 2 cloves garlic, minced
- 1 pint grape tomatoes, halved, or 2½ cups chopped tomatoes
- ½ cup dry white wine
- 2 Tbsp. capers, rinsed
- ½ tsp. salt
- ½ tsp. black pepper
- 2 tsp. cold unsalted butter, cubed
- 2 Tbsp. chopped fresh basil
- 1 lb. skinless, boneless chicken breast halves
- 1 Tbsp. olive oil

**1.** In a large skillet heat 1½ tsp. oil over medium. Add garlic; cook and stir 30 seconds. Stir in tomatoes, wine, capers, and ¼ tsp. each of the salt and pepper; cook about 4 minutes or until the liquid has evaporated slightly. Stir in butter; cook and stir 1 to 2 minutes or until the sauce has thickened slightly and the tomatoes are soft. Stir in basil. Remove from heat; keep warm.
**2.** Using the flat side of a meat mallet, flatten chicken between two pieces of plastic wrap to ½ inch thick. Rub with oil and sprinkle with the remaining ¼ tsp. each salt and pepper.
**3.** Grill chicken, covered, over medium-high 8 to 10 minutes or until done (165°F), turning once. Serve chicken with sauce.

**PER SERVING** (4 oz. chicken + ½ cup sauce each) **CAL** 232, **FAT** 10 g (3 g sat. fat), **CHOL** 68 mg, **SODIUM** 398 mg, **CARB** 6 g (2 g fiber, 3 g sugars), **PRO** 24 g

Sheet-Pan
Orange-
Apricot
Drumsticks

### Spicy Chicken and Snow Pea Skillet

**23g**
**CARB**

SERVES 4
TOTAL 25 min.

- 1  lb. skinless, boneless chicken breast, cut into ¾-inch pieces
- 1  to 2 tsp. harissa paste
- 2  cloves garlic, minced
- 1  Tbsp. olive oil
- 2  cups cherry tomatoes, halved
- 12  oz. snow pea pods, trimmed
- 1  15-oz. can no-salt-added garbanzo beans (chickpeas), rinsed and drained
- ½  cup reduced-sodium chicken broth
- ¼  tsp. salt
- 1  lemon
- ⅓  cup chopped fresh parsley
- ¼  cup pitted Kalamata olives, halved
- ¼  cup plain fat-free Greek yogurt
- 4  1-oz. slices French bread, toasted (optional)

**1.** In a medium bowl combine chicken, harissa paste, and garlic; toss to coat. In an extra-large skillet heat oil over medium-high. Add chicken; cook and stir until no longer pink. Remove from skillet.

**2.** In the same skillet combine the next five ingredients (through salt). Bring to boiling; reduce heat. Cover and simmer, about 5 minutes or until tomatoes are softened and pea pods are tender. Return chicken to skillet.

**3.** Meanwhile, remove 1 tsp. zest and squeeze 1 Tbsp. juice from lemon. Stir zest, juice, parsley, and olives into chicken mixture. Top servings with yogurt and, if desired, serve with bread for dipping.

**PER SERVING** (2 cups each) **CAL** 323, **FAT** 10 g (1 g sat. fat), **CHOL** 83 mg, **SODIUM** 502 mg, **CARB** 23 g (7 g fiber, 7 g sugars), **PRO** 35 g

## Lemon Chicken and Rice

**29g CARB**

**SERVES** 8
**HANDS ON** 50 min.
**TOTAL** 1 hr. 35 min.

- Nonstick cooking spray
- 2 Tbsp. olive oil
- 8 skinless, boneless chicken thighs (1¼ to 1½ lb. total), trimmed
- 2 large onions, thinly sliced
- ½ tsp. salt
- 3 cloves garlic, minced
- 2 tsp. ground turmeric
- 1 tsp. paprika
  Generous pinch saffron (optional)
- 3 cups shredded cabbage (about ½ of a small head)
- 4 cups cooked brown rice, preferably basmati or jasmine
- ¼ cup lemon juice
- 2 Tbsp. chopped fresh parsley (optional)
- 1 lemon, sliced (optional)

**1.** Preheat oven to 375°F. Coat two 8-inch square baking dishes or foil pans with cooking spray.

**2.** In a large nonstick skillet heat 1 Tbsp. of the oil over medium-high. Add four chicken thighs; cook about 4 minutes or until both sides are lightly browned, turning once. Transfer the chicken to a plate. Repeat with the remaining chicken thighs. Pour off all but about 1 Tbsp. drippings from the skillet.

**3.** Add the remaining 1 Tbsp. oil and the onions to the skillet; sprinkle with ¼ tsp. of the salt. Cook and stir 12 to 15 minutes or until soft and golden. Stir in garlic, turmeric, paprika, and saffron (if using); cook and stir 2 minutes. Transfer onions to a plate.

**4.** Add cabbage to the skillet. Cook and stir over medium-high about 3 minutes or until wilted. Stir in rice, lemon juice, the remaining ¼ tsp. salt, and half of the reserved onion. Continue cooking 5 to 7 minutes or until rice is well coated and heated through.

**5.** Divide rice mixture between the prepared baking dishes; nestle four of the chicken thighs in each dish. Top each with half of the remaining cooked onions. Cover both dishes with foil. Label one and freeze up to 1 month.

**6.** Bake the remaining casserole, covered, 30 minutes. Uncover and continue baking 5 to 10 minutes or until

Lemon Chicken and Rice

chicken is done (165°F) and onions are starting to brown around the edges. If desired, garnish with parsley and lemon slices.

**TIP** If you're serving a crowd, prepare as directed, but place the full recipe in a 13×9-inch baking pan. Bake, covered, 10 minutes more. Uncover, and continue as directed.

**PER SERVING** (1 thigh + 1 cup rice mixture each) **CAL** 274, **FAT** 10 g (2 g sat. fat), **CHOL** 50 mg, **SODIUM** 194 mg, **CARB** 29 g (3 g fiber, 3 g sugars), **PRO** 17 g

## QUICK TIP

Thaw frozen casserole overnight in the refrigerator. Bake as directed, except bake 10 minutes more after uncovering.

Greek
Chicken with
Roasted
Spring
Vegetables

## Greek Chicken with Roasted Spring Vegetables

**17g CARB**

SERVES 4
HANDS ON 25 min.
TOTAL 45 min.

Nonstick olive oil cooking spray
2 8-oz. skinless, boneless chicken breast halves, cut in half crosswise
3 Tbsp. buttermilk
6 cloves garlic, minced
½ cup panko
2 Tbsp. grated Parmesan cheese
½ tsp. kosher salt
½ tsp. black pepper
2 cups 1-inch pieces asparagus
1½ cups sliced fresh cremini mushrooms
1½ cups halved grape tomatoes
1 tsp. olive oil
1 recipe Lemon Vinaigrette
Chopped fresh dill

**1.** Place a 15×10-inch baking pan in oven. Preheat oven to 475°F. Lightly coat another 15×10-inch baking pan with cooking spray.
**2.** Meanwhile, using the flat side of a meat mallet, flatten chicken between two pieces of plastic wrap until ½ inch thick.
**3.** Place chicken in a medium bowl. Add buttermilk and two of the minced garlic cloves; stir to coat. In a shallow dish stir together panko, cheese, and ¼ tsp. each of the salt and pepper. Dip chicken into panko mixture, turning to coat. Lightly coat both sides of chicken with cooking spray. Arrange chicken on sprayed baking pan.
**4.** In a large bowl combine asparagus, mushrooms, tomatoes, oil, the remaining four cloves minced garlic, and ¼ tsp. each salt and pepper.
**5.** Carefully place asparagus mixture on the preheated pan. Place both baking pans in oven. Roast 15 to 18 minutes or until chicken is done (165°F) and vegetables are tender. To serve, drizzle chicken and vegetables with Lemon Vinaigrette and top with dill.

**LEMON VINAIGRETTE** Remove ½ tsp. zest and squeeze 1 Tbsp. juice from 1 lemon. In a small bowl whisk together lemon zest and juice, 1 Tbsp. each olive oil and reduced-fat crumbled feta cheese, and ½ tsp. honey.

Turkey Sausage and Zucchini Lasagna

**PER SERVING** *(3½ oz. chicken + ½ cup vegetables each)* **CAL** 272, **FAT** 9 g *(2 g sat. fat)*, **CHOL** 87 mg, **SODIUM** 295 mg, **CARB** 17 g *(3 g fiber, 6 g sugars)*, **PRO** 31 g

## Turkey Sausage and Zucchini Lasagna

**27g CARB**

SERVES 8
HANDS ON 45 min.
TOTAL 1 hr. 35 min.

Nonstick cooking spray
8 oz. sweet Italian turkey sausage links, such as Jennie-O (2 to 3 links)
1 10-oz. bag fresh spinach
1 28-oz. can no-salt-added tomato sauce
8 sheets no-boil lasagna noodles
1 cup part-skim ricotta cheese
1 cup shredded part-skim mozzarella cheese
3 small or 2 medium zucchini (24 oz. total), trimmed and thinly sliced lengthwise into long strips
½ cup freshly grated Parmesan cheese (2 oz.)

**1.** Preheat oven to 375°F. Coat two 8-inch square baking dishes with cooking spray.
**2.** Remove and discard sausage casings; crumble the sausage into a medium nonstick skillet. Cook over medium about 3 minutes or until cooked through, stirring to break up the meat. Transfer sausage to a plate.

**3.** Add spinach to the pan; cook and stir over medium-high about 3 minutes or until just wilted. Transfer to a colander to drain. When cool enough to handle, squeeze out any excess water and coarsely chop.
**4.** To assemble the lasagnas, spread ⅓ cup tomato sauce over the bottom of each prepared baking dish. Top each with a layer of 2 lasagna sheets and spread with another ⅓ cup of the sauce. Top each with 2 Tbsp. each ricotta and mozzarella, then scatter 2 Tbsp. of the spinach and 2 Tbsp. of the sausage over the tops. Add another layer of zucchini slices, then ⅓ cup of the sauce and 2 Tbsp. each of the ricotta, mozzarella, spinach, and sausage. Repeat these layers two more times (first with the pasta, then with the zucchini). Top each lasagna with ¼ cup Parmesan. Coat two pieces of foil with cooking spray and cover both pans with foil. Label and freeze one lasagna up to 1 month.*
**5.** Bake the second lasagna, covered, about 30 minutes or until bubbling. Uncover and bake 10 to 15 minutes more or until the cheeses begin to turn golden. Let stand 5 minutes before cutting. Cut into four 4-inch squares.

**\*TIP** Thaw frozen lasagna overnight in the refrigerator. Bake as directed.

**PER SERVING** *(one 4-inch square each)* **CAL** 262, **FAT** 10 g *(5 g sat. fat)*, **CHOL** 47 mg, **SODIUM** 442 mg, **CARB** 27 g *(4 g fiber, 8 g sugars)*, **PRO** 19 g

## Grilled Pork Tenderloin with Stone-Fruit Salsa

**8g**
**CARB**

| | |
|---|---|
| SERVES | 4 |
| HANDS ON | 25 min. |
| TOTAL | 45 min. |

- 1 **medium peach, halved and pitted**
- 1 **medium purple plum, halved and pitted**
- 1 **medium apricot, halved and pitted**
- 1 **1-inch-thick slice red onion**
- 2 **Tbsp. olive oil**
- ¾ **tsp. salt**
- 1 **tsp. black pepper**
- 2 **Tbsp. chopped fresh cilantro**
- 1 **Tbsp. lime juice**
- 2 **cloves garlic, minced**
- ¾ **tsp. chili powder**
- ½ **tsp. ground cumin**
- 1 **lb. pork tenderloin, trimmed**

**1.** For salsa, brush fruit halves and onion slice with 1 Tbsp. of the oil. Sprinkle with ¼ tsp. each of the pepper and salt. Grill the fruit and onion, covered, over medium 6 to 8 minutes or until tender and grill-marked, turning once. Coarsely chop fruit. Transfer to a medium bowl; stir in cilantro and lime juice.

**2.** In a small bowl combine the remaining 1 Tbsp. oil, the garlic, chili powder, cumin, and the remaining ¾ tsp. pepper and ½ tsp. salt; rub evenly over pork. Grill the pork, covered, over medium 14 to 16 minutes or until 145°F, turning every 1½ minutes.

**3.** Transfer pork to a cutting board. Cover with foil; let stand 5 minutes before slicing. Slice the pork diagonally. Serve pork with salsa.

**PER SERVING** *(3 oz. pork + about ½ cup salsa each)* **CAL** 219, **FAT** 10 g *(2 g sat. fat)*, **CHOL** 74 mg, **SODIUM** 512 mg, **CARB** 8 g *(1 g fiber, 6 g sugars)*, **PRO** 25 g

Grilled Pork Tenderloin with Stone-Fruit Salsa

BLT Pizza

## BLT Pizza

**55g**
**CARB**

SERVES 4
HANDS ON 20 min.
TOTAL 1 hr.

Nonstick cooking spray
1 cup all-purpose flour
1 cup white whole wheat flour
1 pkg. active dry yeast
¼ tsp. salt
⅔ cup warm water (105°F to 115°F)
1 Tbsp. olive oil
1 Tbsp. cornmeal
3 to 4 roma tomatoes, thinly sliced
½ cup thinly sliced red onion
3 slices lower-sodium, less-fat bacon, crisp-cooked and crumbled
1 cup shredded part-skim mozzarella cheese (4 oz.)

3 cups baby arugula
1 Tbsp. balsamic glaze

**1.** Coat a medium bowl with cooking spray. In a food processor* combine both flours, the yeast, and salt. With processor running, add the warm water and oil until mixture forms a ball. Remove and shape dough into a smooth ball. Place in the prepared bowl, turning to grease surface of dough. Cover and let rise in a warm place until double in size (30 to 45 minutes).
**2.** Preheat oven to 450°F. Coat a baking sheet with cooking spray; sprinkle with cornmeal. On a lightly floured surface roll and stretch dough into a 12×8-inch oval or rectangle. Place on the prepared baking sheet.

**3.** Bake 8 minutes. Remove crust from oven. Arrange tomatoes, onion, and bacon on crust. Sprinkle with cheese. Bake about 8 minutes more or until crust is golden and cheese is bubbly.
**4.** Top with arugula; let stand 5 minutes. Drizzle with balsamic glaze.

*TIP If you prefer not to use a food processor, in a large bowl stir together both flours, yeast, and salt; stir in the warm water and oil until moistened. Turn dough out onto a lightly floured surface. Knead until smooth and elastic (about 3 minutes). Let rise and continue as directed.

PER SERVING (1 portion each) **CAL** 378, **FAT** 11 g (4 g sat. fat), **CHOL** 20 mg, **SODIUM** 384 mg, **CARB** 55 g (6 g fiber, 4 g sugars), **PRO** 18 g

Thai-Inspired Pork and Rice Noodles with Cucumbers

## Thai-Inspired Pork and Rice Noodles with Cucumbers

**38g**
**CARB**

SERVES 4
TOTAL 40 min.

- 4 tsp. honey
- 1 Tbsp. fish sauce
- 1 Tbsp. chili-garlic sauce
- 2 Tbsp. olive oil
- 1 lb. thin boneless pork chops, trimmed and cut into ¼-inch strips
- 6 green onions, sliced, white and green parts separated
- 1½ Tbsp. minced fresh garlic
- 1½ Tbsp. grated fresh ginger
- ¼ tsp. black pepper
- 4 oz. dried vermicelli rice noodles
- 2 cups thinly sliced English cucumber
- 1½ cups fresh bean sprouts
- 1 cup matchstick-cut or shredded carrot
- ¼ cup chopped fresh mint
- ¼ cup chopped fresh cilantro
- 2 Tbsp. lime juice
  Lime wedges

**1.** In a small bowl stir together honey, fish sauce, and chili-garlic sauce.
**2.** In a large nonstick skillet or wok heat oil over medium. Add pork, green onion whites, garlic, ginger, and pepper; cook about 3 minutes or until pork is no longer pink, stirring occasionally. Add the honey mixture, stirring to scrape up any browned bits from bottom of the pan. Reduce heat to medium-low; cook about 2 minutes more or until the pork is just cooked through. Remove from heat.
**3.** Cook rice noodles according to package directions. Reserve 1 cup of the cooking water; drain the noodles.
**4.** Add the noodles, the remaining green onions, and the next six ingredients (through lime juice); toss to coat. Stir in enough of the reserved cooking water, ¼ cup at a time, until the mixture is saucy and loose.
**5.** Divide the pork and noodle mixture among bowls and, if desired, garnish with additional mint. Serve with lime wedges.

**PER SERVING** (2 cups each) **CAL** 375, **FAT** 13 g (3 g sat. fat), **CHOL** 57 mg, **SODIUM** 495 mg, **CARB** 38 g (4 g fiber, 12 g sugars), **PRO** 25 g

## Apple Pork Stir-Fry

**39g**
**CARB**

SERVES 2
TOTAL 25 min.

- 2 Tbsp. unsweetened apple juice
- 1½ Tbsp. apple jelly
- 2 tsp. reduced-sodium soy sauce
- 2 tsp. reduced-sodium teriyaki sauce
- ⅛ to ¼ tsp. crushed red pepper
  Nonstick cooking spray
- 1 small red bell pepper, cut into bite-size strips (½ cup)
- ¼ cup sliced onion
- ¼ cup sliced celery
- ¼ cup matchstick-size apple strips
- 2 Tbsp. canned sliced water chestnuts, drained
- 2 Tbsp. shredded carrot
- 1 tsp. grated fresh ginger
- 1 clove garlic, minced
- 2 tsp. sesame oil
- 6 oz. boneless pork top loin chops, cut into thin bite-size strips
- ⅔ cup hot cooked brown rice

**1.** For sauce, in a small bowl combine the first five ingredients (through crushed red pepper).
**2.** Meanwhile, coat an unheated large nonstick skillet or wok with cooking spray. Heat skillet over medium-high. Add bell pepper, onion, and celery to hot skillet. Cover and cook 3 minutes, stirring occasionally. Add apple, water chestnuts, carrot, ginger, and garlic; cover and cook 3 to 4 minutes more or until vegetables and apple are crisp-tender, stirring occasionally. Remove vegetable mixture from skillet.
**3.** Add sesame oil to the same skillet. Add pork strips. Cook and stir over medium-high 2 to 3 minutes or until cooked through. Return vegetable mixture to skillet; add sauce mixture. Cook and stir 1 to 2 minutes or until heated through. Serve stir-fry mixture with hot cooked rice.

**PER SERVING** (1 cup pork mixture + ⅓ cup rice each) **CAL** 294, **FAT** 7 g (1 g sat. fat), **CHOL** 35 mg, **SODIUM** 498 mg, **CARB** 39 g (4 g fiber, 16 g sugars), **PRO** 20 g

Apple Pork
Stir-Fry

Stuffed
Zucchini
Parmesan

## Stuffed Zucchini Parmesan

**23g**
CARB

SERVES 6
HANDS ON 30 min.
TOTAL 1 hr.

- 3 tsp. olive oil
- ½ cup finely chopped onion
- 2 cloves garlic, minced
- 1 28-oz. can crushed tomatoes
- ¼ tsp. honey
- ¼ tsp. salt
- ⅛ tsp. black pepper
- 2 Tbsp. chopped fresh basil or 2 tsp. dried basil, crushed
- 6 medium zucchini, halved lengthwise*
- 1 lb. 90%-lean ground beef
- 1 Tbsp. dried Italian seasoning
- ¾ cup grated Parmesan cheese
- 6 Tbsp. shredded part-skim mozzarella cheese

**1.** Preheat oven to 400°F. If desired, line a large rimmed baking sheet with foil or parchment paper and coat with *nonstick cooking spray.*
**2.** For sauce, in a large saucepan heat 2 tsp. of the oil over medium-high. Add onion; cook and stir about 5 minutes or until tender. Add garlic; cook and stir 30 seconds. Stir in tomatoes, honey, salt, pepper, and dried basil (if using). Bring to boiling; reduce heat. Simmer, uncovered, 20 minutes, stirring occasionally. Stir in fresh basil (if using).
**3.** Meanwhile, score the cut side of each zucchini half in a crisscross pattern, taking care not to cut through the skin. Place the halves, cut sides down, on the prepared baking sheet. Bake 20 minutes. Let cool.
**4.** In a medium skillet heat the remaining 1 tsp. oil over medium. Add ground beef and Italian seasoning. Cook about 5 minutes or until no longer pink. Add to the tomato mixture in saucepan.
**5.** When the zucchini are cool enough to handle, use a spoon to carefully scoop out the center of each half, leaving about a ½-inch-thick shell. Chop the scooped-out zucchini and add it to the sauce mixture. Place zucchini halves, cut sides up, on the baking sheet.
**6.** Spoon about ⅓ cup of the sauce mixture into each zucchini half. Sprinkle 1 Tbsp. Parmesan and 1½ tsp. mozzarella on each zucchini half. Bake stuffed zucchini about 20 minutes or until heated through and golden brown.

Grilled Steak with Chimichurri

**\*TIP** Use long straight zucchini, which are easier to hollow out for stuffing, for this dish.

**PER SERVING** *(2 stuffed zucchini halves each)* **CAL** 318, **FAT** 15 g *(6 g sat. fat)*, **CHOL** 62 mg, **SODIUM** 645 mg, **CARB** 23 g *(5 g fiber, 13 g sugars)*, **PRO** 26 g

---

## Grilled Steak with Chimichurri

**1g**
CARB

SERVES 4
TOTAL 30 min.

- ¼ cup packed fresh parsley leaves, chopped
- 1½ tsp. fresh oregano leaves, chopped
- 1 medium clove garlic, minced
- 2 tsp. olive oil
- 2 tsp. red wine vinegar
- 2 tsp. lemon juice
- ⅛ tsp. crushed red pepper
- ½ tsp. salt
- 1 lb. beef hanger or flank steak

**1.** For chimichurri sauce, in a small bowl stir together the first seven ingredients (through crushed red pepper) and ¼ tsp. of the salt.
**2.** Preheat grill to medium-high. Rub 1 Tbsp. of the sauce over the steak; sprinkle with the remaining ¼ tsp. salt. Grill the steak, covered, over medium-high 6 to 8 minutes or until desired doneness (145°F for medium-rare), turning once.
**3.** Transfer steak to a cutting board. Cover with foil; let steak stand 5 minutes. Thinly slice steak across the grain. Serve steak with the remaining chimichurri sauce.

**TO MAKE AHEAD** Prepare chimichurri sauce as directed in Step 1. Cover and refrigerate up to 1 day.

**PER SERVING** *(3 oz. steak + about 1 Tbsp. sauce each)* **CAL** 196, **FAT** 10 g *(4 g sat. fat)*, **CHOL** 68 mg, **SODIUM** 338 mg, **CARB** 1 g *(0 g fiber, 0 g sugars)*, **PRO** 23 g

Italian
Meatballs
with Roasted
Green Beans
and Potatoes

## Italian Meatballs with Roasted Green Beans and Potatoes

**31g**
**CARB**

| SERVES 4 |
| HANDS ON 35 min. |
| TOTAL 55 min. |

- 1 lb. small red potatoes, quartered
- 4 tsp. olive oil
- 4 cloves garlic, minced
- 1 tsp. chopped fresh rosemary
- 1 tsp. kosher salt
- ¾ tsp. black pepper
- 6 Tbsp. quick-cooking rolled oats
- 1 egg white
- ¼ cup grated onion
- 1 tsp. dried Italian seasoning, crushed
- ¼ tsp. crushed red pepper
- 12 oz. 90%-lean ground beef
- 8 oz. fresh green beans, trimmed
- ¼ cup heart-healthy pasta sauce, such as Prego Heart Smart
- 2 Tbsp. freshly grated Parmesan cheese
- 2 tsp. coarsely chopped fresh basil

**1.** Preheat oven to 425°F. Place potatoes in a 15×10-inch baking pan. Drizzle with 2 tsp. of the oil and sprinkle with 2 of the garlic cloves, the rosemary, ½ tsp. of the salt, and ¼ tsp. of the black pepper; toss to coat. Roast 10 minutes.

**2.** Meanwhile, place oats in a food processor. Cover; process to a coarse powder. In a large bowl combine oat powder, egg white, onion, Italian seasoning, crushed red pepper, one of the garlic cloves, and ¼ tsp. each of the salt and black pepper. Add beef; mix well. Using ¼ cup of the mixture for each, shape into eight meatballs.

**3.** In a medium bowl combine the remaining 2 tsp. oil, 1 clove garlic, and ¼ tsp. each salt and black pepper. Add green beans; toss to coat.

**4.** Push potatoes to one end of the baking pan. Arrange meatballs in the other end and mound beans in the center of the pan.

**5.** Roast 20 to 25 minutes more or until meatballs are done (160°F) and vegetables are tender, rotating the pan after 10 minutes and spooning pasta sauce over meatballs the last 2 to 3 minutes of roasting.

**6.** Sprinkle meatballs with Parmesan cheese and basil. If desired, serve with additional pasta sauce.

**PER SERVING** *(2 meatballs + ¾ cup potatoes + ½ cup beans each)* **CAL** 348, **FAT** 15 g *(5 g sat. fat)*, **CHOL** 54 mg, **SODIUM** 465 mg, **CARB** 31 g *(5 g fiber, 5 g sugars)*, **PRO** 23 g

## Chipotle Beef Tacos

**25g CARB**

**SERVES** 8
**HANDS ON** 35 min.
**TOTAL** 40 min.

Nonstick cooking spray
1 cup chopped onion
6 cloves garlic, coarsely chopped
¾ cup 50%-less-sodium beef broth
⅓ cup no-salt-added tomato paste
¼ cup cider vinegar
1 tsp. dried oregano, crushed
1 tsp. ground cumin
½ tsp. ground chipotle chile pepper
½ tsp. black pepper
¼ tsp. salt
2 lb. 93%-lean ground beef or turkey
16 6-inch white corn tortillas, warmed
1 recipe Tomato-Avocado Pico de Gallo

**1.** Coat an extra-large nonstick skillet with cooking spray; heat over medium. Add onion and garlic; cook about 5 minutes or just until onion is tender, stirring occasionally. Transfer onion mixture to a blender or food processor. Add the next eight ingredients (through salt). Cover and blend or process until smooth.

**2.** In the same skillet cook ground beef over medium-high until browned. Drain off fat. Add onion mixture to meat in skillet. Cook and stir over medium just until bubbly; reduce heat. Simmer, covered, 5 minutes, stirring occasionally.

**3.** Serve meat mixture in warm tortillas with Tomato-Avocado Pico de Gallo.

**TOMATO-AVOCADO PICO DE GALLO** In a medium bowl gently stir together 2 cups chopped tomatoes, 1 cup peeled and chopped avocado, ½ cup chopped fresh cilantro, and, if desired, ⅛ to ¼ tsp. crushed red pepper.

**PER SERVING** *(2 tacos each)* **CAL** 323, **FAT** 12 g *(4 g sat. fat)*, **CHOL** 71 mg, **SODIUM** 200 mg, **CARB** 25 g *(4 g fiber, 4 g sugars)*, **PRO** 27 g

## Shrimp and Pea Pod Stir-Fry

**32g** | **SERVES** 4
**CARB** | **TOTAL** 30 min.

- 1 lb. fresh or frozen medium shrimp in shells
- ½ cup reduced-sodium chicken broth
- 1 Tbsp. reduced-sodium soy sauce
- 2 tsp. cornstarch
- 2 tsp. grated fresh ginger
- 2 tsp. sesame oil
- 3 cloves garlic, minced
- ¼ tsp. salt
- ¼ tsp. crushed red pepper (optional)
- 2 Tbsp. vegetable oil
- 1 cup sliced onion
- 1 cup matchstick-cut carrots
- 12 oz. snow pea pods, trimmed
- 1⅓ cups hot cooked brown rice

**1.** Thaw shrimp, if frozen. Peel and devein shrimp, leaving tails intact if desired. For sauce, in a small bowl combine the next eight ingredients (through crushed red pepper if using).
**2.** In an extra-large skillet or a wok heat oil over medium-high. Add onion and carrots; cook and stir 3 to 4 minutes or just until beginning to soften. Add pea pods; cook and stir 3 minutes. Add shrimp; cook and stir about 3 minutes more or just until shrimp are opaque. Add sauce; cook and stir until thick and bubbly. Serve shrimp mixture over rice.

**PER SERVING** *(1 ½ cups shrimp mixture + ⅓ cup rice each)* **CAL** 323, **FAT** 11 g *(1 g sat. fat),* **CHOL** 159 mg, **SODIUM** 499 mg, **CARB** 32 g *(5 g fiber, 7 g sugars),* **PRO** 26 g

Shrimp and Pea Pod Stir-Fry

Italian
Penne and
Tuna

## Italian Penne with Tuna

**41g**
**CARB**

**SERVES** 2
**TOTAL** 20 min.

- 3 oz. dried multigrain penne pasta
- 1 Tbsp. olive oil
- ¾ cup thinly sliced leeks (white parts only)
- 2 cloves garlic, minced
- 4 cups fresh baby spinach
- 1 2.6-oz. pouch albacore tuna in water, broken into large chunks
- 3 Tbsp. reduced-calorie Italian salad dressing
- 2 Tbsp. dried tomatoes (not oil-packed), chopped
  Cracked black pepper (optional)

**1.** In a large saucepan cook pasta according to package directions; drain. Return to saucepan.

**2.** Meanwhile, in a large skillet heat oil over medium-low. Add leeks and garlic; cook 5 to 7 minutes or until tender, stirring occasionally. Remove from heat. Add spinach; stir until slightly wilted.

**3.** Stir spinach mixture into pasta. Add tuna, Italian dressing, and dried tomatoes; toss gently to combine. If desired, sprinkle with pepper.

**PER SERVING** (1½ cups each) **CAL** 307, **FAT** 11 g (1 g sat. fat), **CHOL** 13 mg, **SODIUM** 426 mg, **CARB** 41 g (7 g fiber, 6 g sugars), **PRO** 16 g

Almond-
Tomato
Pesto Pasta
and Zoodles
with Salmon

## Almond-Tomato Pesto Pasta and Zoodles with Salmon

**41g CARB** | SERVES 6
TOTAL 35 min.

- 2 medium zucchini (1¾ lb. total)
- 1 tsp. salt
- ½ cup raw whole almonds, toasted
- 3 cups grape tomatoes (1 lb.)
- 1 cup packed fresh basil leaves + ¼ cup chopped fresh basil
- 2 to 4 cloves garlic
- ¼ tsp. crushed red pepper
- 3 Tbsp. olive oil
- 8 oz. dried whole wheat spaghetti
- 4 4-oz. salmon fillets, skin removed
- ¼ tsp. black pepper
- 2 Tbsp. grated Parmesan cheese (optional)

**1.** Using a spiralizer or vegetable peeler, cut zucchini into long thin strips. Place in a colander set over a large bowl. Sprinkle zucchini with ¼ tsp. of the salt; toss to combine. Let drain 15 minutes.
**2.** Meanwhile, for pesto, in a food processor pulse almonds until coarsely chopped. Add tomatoes, the 1 cup basil leaves, the garlic, and crushed red pepper; pulse until coarsely chopped. Add 2 Tbsp. of the oil and ½ tsp. of the salt; pulse until combined.
**3.** Cook spaghetti according to package directions; drain. Place spaghetti in a large bowl. Gently squeeze the zucchini to remove excess liquid; add to the bowl with the spaghetti.
**4.** In a large skillet heat the remaining 1 Tbsp. oil over medium-high until shimmering. Sprinkle black pepper and the remaining ¼ tsp. salt over salmon. Cook salmon in hot oil about 4 minutes or until the bottoms are golden and crispy. Turn salmon; cook 2 to 4 minutes more or until fish flakes easily. Transfer salmon to a plate and use a fork to gently flake.
**5.** Add the pesto to the spaghetti mixture; toss to coat. Gently stir in the salmon. Top with the remaining ¼ cup chopped fresh basil. If desired, sprinkle with Parmesan and additional black pepper.

**PER SERVING** *(1 ½ cups each)* **CAL** 450, **FAT** 24 g *(4 g sat. fat)*, **CHOL** 42 mg, **SODIUM** 459 mg, **CARB** 41 g *(7 g fiber, 5 g sugars)*, **PRO** 26 g

## Grilled Salmon with Cilantro-Ginger Sauce

**2g CARB** | SERVES 4
TOTAL 25 min.

- 2 Tbsp. toasted sesame oil
- 1 Tbsp. fresh lime juice
- 1 Tbsp. chopped fresh cilantro
- 1 tsp. fish sauce
- 1 tsp. finely chopped Thai red pepper or fresh jalapeño pepper (tip, p. 154)
- 1 tsp. grated fresh ginger
- 1 tsp. honey
- 1 medium clove garlic, mashed into paste
- 1 lb. skin-on salmon fillet (about 2 inches thick), cut into 4 portions
- ½ tsp. black pepper
- ¼ tsp. salt

**1.** For cilantro-ginger sauce, in a small bowl whisk together 1 Tbsp. of the oil and the next seven ingredients (through garlic). Reserve 1 Tbsp. of the sauce.
**2.** Pat salmon dry with paper towels. Rub the remaining 1 Tbsp. oil on both sides of the salmon. Sprinkle both sides with black pepper and salt. Grill salmon, skin sides up, covered, over medium-high about 6 minutes or until the salmon lifts from the grates without sticking. Turn salmon and brush with the reserved 1 Tbsp. sauce. Grill 1 to 2 minutes more or until the salmon lifts from the grates without sticking and flakes easily. Serve with the remaining sauce.

**PER SERVING** *(3 oz. salmon + about 2 tsp. sauce each)* **CAL** 204, **FAT** 11 g *(2 g sat. fat)*, **CHOL** 53 mg, **SODIUM** 320 mg, **CARB** 2 g *(0 g fiber, 2 g sugars)*, **PRO** 23 g

Grilled
Salmon with
Cilantro-
Ginger
Sauce

Mango-
Lime Fish
Tacos

## Mango-Lime Fish Tacos

**35g CARB** | **SERVES** 8
**TOTAL** 30 min.

- 2 lb. fresh or frozen skinless tilapia or sole fillets
- ½ tsp. salt
- ½ tsp. garlic powder
- ¼ tsp. black pepper
- 2 limes, thinly sliced
- 2 tsp. canola oil
- ½ of a medium onion, thinly sliced
- 1 tsp. cumin seeds
- 6 cups coarsely shredded red and/or green cabbage
- 16 6-inch white corn tortillas, warmed
- 2 cups chopped fresh mangoes
- 1½ cups crumbled Cotija cheese (6 oz.)
- ¾ cup light sour cream
  Radishes, cut into thin strips
  Lime wedges
  Sriracha sauce

**1.** Thaw fish, if frozen. Preheat oven to 425°F. Line an extra-large baking sheet with parchment paper.
**2.** Arrange fish in a single layer on the prepared baking sheet. Sprinkle with ¼ tsp. of the salt, the garlic powder, and pepper. Top with lime slices. Bake 5 to 8 minutes or until fish flakes easily.
**3.** Meanwhile, in a large nonstick skillet heat oil over medium. Add onion, cumin seeds, and the remaining ¼ tsp. salt. Cook and stir about 30 seconds or until cumin is fragrant. Gradually add cabbage, tossing with tongs to combine. Cook 3 to 4 minutes or just until cabbage is softened.
**4.** Coarsely flake fish. Serve cabbage mixture in warm tortillas topped with fish, mangoes, cheese, sour cream, and radishes. Serve with lime wedges and sriracha sauce.

**PER SERVING** (2 tacos each) **CAL** 373, **FAT** 13 g (6 g sat. fat), **CHOL** 84 mg, **SODIUM** 575 mg, **CARB** 35 g (6 g fiber, 11 g sugars), **PRO** 31 g

---

## Spinach and Herb Galette

**26g CARB** | **SERVES** 6
**HANDS ON** 30 min.
**TOTAL** 2 hr. 20 min.

- ¾ cup all-purpose flour
- ½ cup whole wheat flour
- 1 tsp. black pepper

Spinach and Herb Galette

- ¾ tsp. salt
- 5 Tbsp. olive oil
- 3 to 4 Tbsp. ice water
- 1 lemon
- ⅔ cup fat-free ricotta cheese
- 2 large egg whites
- 2 Tbsp. chopped fresh dill
- 2 Tbsp. chopped fresh oregano
- ½ cup chopped onion
- 4 cloves garlic, minced
- 1 10-oz. pkg. baby spinach
- 1 tsp. grated Parmesan cheese
- 3 Tbsp. crumbled feta cheese

**1.** In a large bowl stir together all-purpose flour, whole wheat flour, pepper, and ½ tsp. of the salt. Drizzle 4½ Tbsp. of the oil over the flour mixture; use your fingertips to rub the flour and oil together until the mixture turns crumbly. Sprinkle 1 Tbsp. of the ice water over part of the mixture; toss gently with a fork. Push the moistened dough to the side of the bowl. Repeat moistening the flour mixture, using 1 Tbsp. ice water at a time, until the mixture is evenly moistened. Form the dough into a ball and wrap in plastic wrap. Chill 1 to 2 hours.
**2.** Preheat oven to 400°F. Line a large rimmed baking sheet with parchment paper.

**3.** Remove 1 tsp. zest and squeeze 1 Tbsp. juice from lemon. In a small bowl stir together zest, juice, ricotta, one of the egg whites, the dill, and oregano.
**4.** In a large nonstick skillet heat the remaining 1½ tsp. oil over medium-high. Add onion and garlic; cook and stir 3 to 5 minutes or until tender. Stir in the remaining ¼ tsp. salt. Add spinach; cook and stir 3 to 4 minutes or until wilted. Spoon into a mesh strainer; press with the back of a spoon to remove excess liquid.
**5.** Unwrap the dough and place on a lightly floured surface. Roll into a 12-inch circle; place on the prepared baking sheet. Spoon the ricotta mixture into center of the dough; spread evenly, leaving a 2-inch border. Top with the spinach mixture. Fold the edges of the dough over to partially cover the filling. Brush dough edges with the remaining egg white and sprinkle with Parmesan.
**6.** Bake 15 minutes. Remove from oven and sprinkle the filling with feta. Bake about 20 minutes more or until crust is browned. Let cool 15 minutes.

**PER SERVING** (1 wedge each) **CAL** 253, **FAT** 13 g (2 g sat. fat), **CHOL** 9 mg, **SODIUM** 422 mg, **CARB** 26 g (3 g fiber, 2 g sugars), **PRO** 9 g

Springtime
Cacio e Pepe

2  medium onions, thinly sliced
3  cloves garlic, minced
1  Tbsp. chili powder
2  tsp. dried oregano
1  tsp. onion powder
1  tsp. ground cumin
1  28-oz. can no-salt-added diced tomatoes
2  15-oz. cans no-salt-added black beans, rinsed and drained
2  4.5-oz. cans diced green chiles
¼  cup chopped fresh cilantro
10  6-inch corn tortillas, quartered
1  cup shredded extra-sharp Cheddar cheese (4 oz.)

**1.** Preheat oven to 375°F. Coat a large baking sheet and two 8-inch square baking dishes with cooking spray.
**2.** Peel the eggplant; cut into ¼-inch-thick slices. Halve the slices (or quarter if large). Arrange eggplant in a single layer on the prepared baking sheet; brush 1 Tbsp. of the oil over the eggplant. Bake 10 to 15 minutes or until eggplant is just beginning to brown on the edges, turning once. Let cool.
**3.** In a large nonstick skillet heat the remaining 1 Tbsp. oil over medium-high. Add onions; cook and stir about 10 minutes or until soft. Add garlic, chili powder, oregano, onion powder, and cumin; cook and stir 30 seconds. Stir in tomatoes, beans, chiles, and cilantro. Remove from heat.
**4.** To assemble the casseroles, cover the bottom of each baking dish with one-fourth of the tortilla pieces each. Spread 1 cup of the tomato-bean mixture over the tortillas, then sprinkle each with ¼ cup cheese. Layer half of the eggplant pieces in each dish; spread each with 1 cup of the tomato-bean mixture. Divide the remaining tortilla pieces and remaining tomato-bean mixture between the casseroles; sprinkle each with ¼ cup cheese. Cover both dishes with foil. Label and freeze one casserole up to 1 month.*
**5.** Bake the remaining casserole, covered, until bubbling, 30 minutes. Uncover; bake about 10 minutes more or until the cheese is lightly browned. Let stand 5 minutes before cutting.

*****TIP** Thaw frozen casserole overnight in the refrigerator. Bake as directed.

**PER SERVING** *(one 4-inch square each)* **CAL** 304, **FAT** 10 g *(3 g sat. fat)*, **CHOL** 13 mg, **SODIUM** 250 mg, **CARB** 41 g *(10 g fiber, 8 g sugars)*, **PRO** 14 g

## Springtime Cacio e Pepe

**32g**
**CARB**

SERVES 4
HANDS ON 15 min.
TOTAL 25 min.

6  oz. dried multigrain spaghetti
8  oz. fresh asparagus, trimmed and cut into 2-inch pieces
1  cup red and/or yellow bell pepper strips (optional)
1  Tbsp. olive oil
2  tsp. lemon zest
½  cup freshly grated Parmesan cheese (2 oz.)
½  to 1 tsp. coarse-ground black pepper
1  cup baby arugula
   Lemon wedges

**1.** Preheat oven to 425°F. In a Dutch oven cook spaghetti according to package directions. Reserve 1 cup of the cooking water; drain the spaghetti. Return spaghetti to Dutch oven.
**2.** Meanwhile, line a 15×10-inch baking pan with foil. Arrange asparagus and pepper strips in the prepared pan and drizzle with oil; toss to coat. Roast 5 to 7 minutes or just until tender. Sprinkle with 1 tsp. of the lemon zest.
**3.** Add ¾ cup of the reserved pasta water, the cheese, and ½ tsp. pepper to spaghetti; stir until creamy. If needed, stir in additional reserved cooking water to reach desired consistency. Add asparagus and arugula; toss to coat. Sprinkle servings with the remaining 1 tsp. lemon zest and ½ tsp. pepper. Serve with lemon wedges.

**PER SERVING** *(1 cup each)* **CAL** 242, **FAT** 9 g *(3 g sat. fat)*, **CHOL** 15 mg, **SODIUM** 225 mg, **CARB** 32 g *(4 g fiber, 3 g sugars)*, **PRO** 13 g

## Eggplant Tortilla Casserole

**41g**
**CARB**

SERVES 8
HANDS ON 30 min.
TOTAL 1 hr. 10 min.

   Nonstick cooking spray
1  medium eggplant (about 1 lb.)
2  Tbsp. canola oil

Eggplant
Tortilla
Casserole

# 2
# MAIN-MEAL
# SALADS

Load up on produce as salad takes center stage. These fresh entrées bring on the greens, vegetables, fruits, and whole grains, as well as meaty proteins. Enjoy colorful, crunchy vegetarian Farro Salad with Kale, hearty Smoky Steak Salad with Arugula and Oranges, and easy Bacon Ranch Salad that's ready in 15.

Mediterranean
Chicken and
Wheat Berry
Salad

## Country-Style
## Wedge Salad with Turkey

**8g**
**CARB**

SERVES 4
TOTAL 25 min.

- 1 large head butterhead lettuce (Bibb or Boston), quartered
- 1 recipe Buttermilk-Avocado Dressing
- 2 cups shredded cooked turkey breast
- 1 cup halved grape or cherry tomatoes
- 2 hard-boiled eggs, chopped
- 4 slices lower-sodium, less-fat bacon, crisp-cooked and crumbled
- ¼ cup finely chopped or sliced red onion
  Cracked black pepper

**1.** Arrange one lettuce quarter on each plate. Drizzle half of the dressing over wedges. Top with turkey, tomatoes, and eggs. Drizzle with the remaining dressing. Sprinkle with bacon, onion, and pepper.

**BUTTERMILK-AVOCADO DRESSING** In a blender combine ¾ cup buttermilk; half of an avocado, peeled and seeded; 1 Tbsp. chopped fresh flat-leaf parsley; ¼ tsp. each onion powder, salt, dry mustard, and black pepper; and 1 clove garlic, minced. Cover and blend until smooth.

**TIP** Avoid added sodium from deli-style turkey by cooking your own turkey breast tenderloins or using leftover roast turkey.

**PER SERVING** (1 wedge salad + ¼ cup dressing each) **CAL** 228, **FAT** 9 g (2 g sat. fat), **CHOL** 149 mg, **SODIUM** 381 mg, **CARB** 8 g (2 g fiber, 5 g sugars), **PRO** 29 g

## Mediterranean Chicken
## and Wheat Berry Salad

**40g**
**CARB**

SERVES 6
HANDS ON 20 min.
SLOW COOK 7 hr. 30 min.
CHILL 4 hr.

- 3 cups reduced-sodium chicken broth
- 1 14.5-oz. can no-salt-added diced fire-roasted tomatoes, undrained
- 1½ cups wheat berries
- ¾ cup chopped cucumber
- ½ cup chopped fresh flat-leaf parsley
- ¼ cup thinly sliced green onions
- 1 Tbsp. chopped fresh mint
- ¼ cup lemon juice
- 1 Tbsp. olive oil
- ½ tsp. ground cumin
- ¼ tsp. garlic salt
- 1 lb. chopped cooked chicken
- ¼ cup crumbled reduced-fat feta cheese (1 oz.)

**1.** In a 4- to 5-qt. slow cooker combine broth, tomatoes, and wheat berries. Cover and cook on low 7½ to 8 hours or until wheat berries are tender.
**2.** Using a slotted spoon, transfer wheat berry mixture to a large bowl. Cool to room temperature. Stir in the next four ingredients (through mint).
**3.** For dressing, in a screw-top jar combine the next four ingredients (through garlic salt). Cover and shake well. Pour dressing over wheat berry mixture; toss gently to coat. Top with chopped cooked chicken. Cover and chill 4 to 24 hours. Sprinkle with cheese before serving.

**PER SERVING** (¾ cup each) **CAL** 368, **FAT** 9 g (2 g sat. fat), **CHOL** 71 mg, **SODIUM** 450 mg, **CARB** 40 g (7 g fiber, 2 g sugars), **PRO** 31 g

Country-
Style
Wedge
Salad with
Turkey

## Spiced Pork Tenderloin with Spinach and Macadamia Nut Salad

**19g CARB**

**SERVES** 4
**HANDS ON** 35 min.
**TOTAL** 55 min.

- 1½ tsp. chili powder
- 1½ tsp. smoked paprika
- 1½ tsp. sweet paprika
- 1½ tsp. garlic powder
- 1½ tsp. onion powder
- ¼ tsp. salt
- ¼ tsp. black pepper
- 1¼ lb. pork tenderloin, trimmed
- 3 Tbsp. olive oil
- 8 cups packed fresh baby spinach
- 1½ cups diced fresh pineapple
- 1 red bell pepper, diced
- ¾ cup chopped unsalted macadamia nuts, toasted
- ¼ cup chopped fresh parsley
- 2 Tbsp. fresh lime juice
- 2 Tbsp. finely chopped shallot
- ¾ tsp. ground coriander
- 1 clove garlic, minced
- ½ tsp. Dijon mustard

**1.** Preheat oven to 450°F. Line a large rimmed baking sheet with foil.
**2.** In a small bowl combine the first seven ingredients (through black pepper). Sprinkle pork with the spice mixture; rub in with your fingers.
**3.** In a large skillet heat 1 Tbsp. of the oil over medium-high. Cook pork in hot oil 4 to 6 minutes or until browned on all sides; transfer pork to the prepared baking sheet.
**4.** Roast 14 to 18 minutes or until pork registers 145°F in the thickest part. Transfer pork to a cutting board. Tent with foil and let rest 10 minutes.
**5.** Meanwhile, in a large bowl combine the next five ingredients (through parsley). For dressing, in a small bowl whisk together the remaining 2 Tbsp. oil and the remaining ingredients.
**6.** Cut the pork into 12 slices. Drizzle dressing over spinach mixture; toss to coat. Arrange salad in serving dishes with pork.

**PER SERVING** *(2¼ cups salad + 3 slices pork each)*
**CAL** 493, **FAT** 33 g *(5 g sat. fat)*, **CHOL** 92 mg,
**SODIUM** 298 mg, **CARB** 19 g *(6 g fiber, 9 g sugars)*,
**PRO** 34 g

Spiced Pork
Tenderloin
with
Spinach and
Macadamia
Nut Salad

Thai-Style
Pork Salad

## Thai-Style Pork Salad

**19g**
**CARB**

**SERVES** 2
**TOTAL** 15 min.

- 4  cups torn romaine lettuce
- 1  cup chopped or sliced cooked pork tenderloin
- ½  cup shredded carrot
- ½  cup shredded red cabbage
- ½  cup fresh snow pea pods, halved
- ¼  cup peanut satay sauce, such as Thai Kitchen
- 1  Tbsp. water
- ¼  cup lightly salted peanuts, chopped
   Chopped fresh Thai basil or basil
   Lime wedges

**1.** In a large bowl combine the first five ingredients (through pea pods).
**2.** For dressing, in a small bowl whisk together satay sauce and the water. Spoon dressing over lettuce mixture; toss to coat. Sprinkle with peanuts and basil and serve with lime wedges.

**PER SERVING** *(3 cups each)* **CAL** 311, **FAT** 15 g *(4 g sat. fat)*, **CHOL** 52 mg, **SODIUM** 322 mg, **CARB** 19 g *(5 g fiber, 9 g sugars)*, **PRO** 25 g

Bacon
Ranch Salad

## Barbecue Chopped Pork Salad

**33g**
**CARB**

SERVES 2
TOTAL 20 min.

- 2 6-inch corn tortillas
  Nonstick cooking spray
- 4 cups chopped romaine lettuce
- 6 oz. roasted lean boneless pork, chopped (1½ cups)
- ½ cup frozen roasted corn, thawed
- ¼ cup thinly sliced red onion
- 2 Tbsp. fat-free milk
- 2 Tbsp. light sour cream
- 2 Tbsp. barbecue sauce

**1.** Preheat oven to 450°F. Cut tortillas into strips. Spread strips on a baking sheet; coat with cooking spray. Bake 5 to 7 minutes or until brown and crisp; cool.

**2.** Divide lettuce, meat, corn, and red onion between bowls. For dressing, in a small bowl whisk together milk, sour cream, and barbecue sauce. Spoon dressing over salads; if desired, toss to coat. Top with tortilla strips.

**TO TOTE** Place lettuce, meat, corn, and red onion in airtight containers. Divide dressing between two small airtight containers. Place tortilla strips in resealable plastic bags. Chill lettuce mixture and dressing overnight. Pack in an insulated bag with a frozen ice pack.

**PER SERVING** (1 salad each) **CAL** 322, **FAT** 7 g (2 g sat. fat), **CHOL** 63 mg, **SODIUM** 243 mg, **CARB** 33 g (5 g fiber, 14 g sugars), **PRO** 33 g

## Bacon Ranch Salad

**19g**
**CARB**

SERVES 2
TOTAL 15 min.

- 4 cups fresh baby spinach
- 1 cup cherry tomatoes, halved
- 2 hard-boiled eggs, sliced
- 4 slices lower-sodium, less-fat bacon, crisp-cooked and crumbled
- 2 Tbsp. shredded sharp cheddar cheese
- 3 Tbsp. light ranch salad dressing
- 1 Tbsp. fat-free milk
- 1 tsp. salt-free Southwest chipotle seasoning, such as Mrs. Dash
- 6 reduced-fat woven wheat crackers, such as Triscuit

**1.** Divide spinach, tomatoes, eggs, bacon, and cheese between bowls.
**2.** For dressing, in a small bowl whisk together ranch dressing, milk, and chipotle seasoning. Drizzle dressing over spinach mixture. Serve with crackers.

**PER SERVING** (2½ cups each) **CAL** 289, **FAT** 15 g (5 g sat. fat), **CHOL** 204 mg, **SODIUM** 600 mg, **CARB** 19 g (4 g fiber, 5 g sugars), **PRO** 16 g

Barbecue
Chopped
Pork Salad

# hearty salads

## How to build a satisfying salad every time.

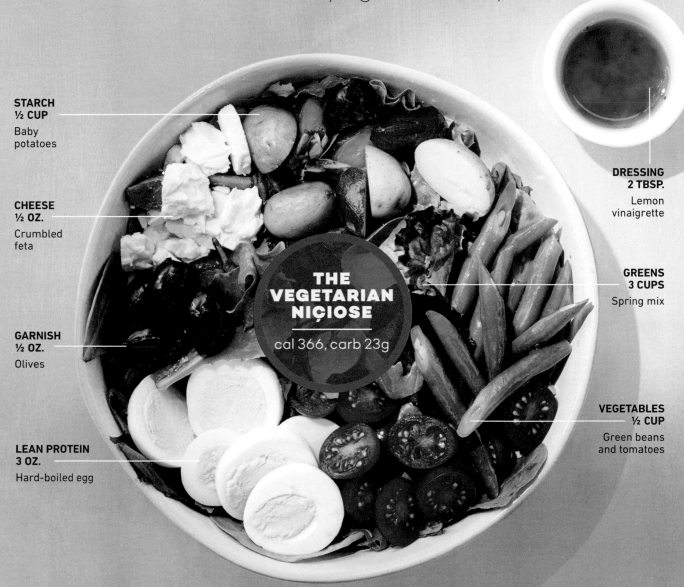

**STARCH**
**½ CUP**
Baby potatoes

**CHEESE**
**½ OZ.**
Crumbled feta

**GARNISH**
**½ OZ.**
Olives

**LEAN PROTEIN**
**3 OZ.**
Hard-boiled egg

**THE VEGETARIAN NIÇIOSE**
cal 366, carb 23g

**DRESSING**
**2 TBSP.**
Lemon vinaigrette

**GREENS**
**3 CUPS**
Spring mix

**VEGETABLES**
**½ CUP**
Green beans and tomatoes

## How it works

You don't need a recipe to make a salad, just a basic formula. Mix and match the categories *(right)* using the amounts shown. Plan ahead and prep your protein, vegetables, and grains or use what's on hand in the fridge. Bonus points for using up vegetable scraps or leftover ingredients that would otherwise go to waste!

**Salad Greens** +
**3 cups**

Escarole
Baby kale
Bibb lettuce
Red leaf lettuce
Romaine
Baby spinach
Spring mix

**Other Produce** +
**½ cup nonstarchy, cooked or raw**

Bell peppers
Carrots
Cucumbers
Green beans
Mushrooms
Radishes
Snap peas
Tomatoes

**Grains or Starch**
**½ cup**

Bulgur
Whole wheat couscous
Farro
Baby potatoes
Quinoa
Winter squash
Sweet potatoes

## Chopped Chicken and Sweet Potato
cal 542, carb 32g

Escarole or romaine, avocado, apples, sweet potato, shredded chicken, cubed cheddar cheese, sunflower seeds, apple cider vinaigrette

### EXPERIMENT!

Try new combos based on what you have on hand or what's on sale.

## Salmon Couscous
cal 464, carb 35g

Spinach, mushrooms, eggplant, whole wheat Israeli couscous, salmon, goat cheese, dried apricots, white wine vinaigrette

## Quinoa Deli
cal 404, carb 39g

Bibb lettuce, red bell peppers, artichoke hearts, quinoa, chickpeas, mozzarella cheese, sliced deli ham, red wine vinaigrette

| + **Lean Protein**<br>3 oz. | + **Cheese**<br>½ oz. | + **Garnish**<br>½ oz. | + **Dressing**<br>2 Tbsp. olive oil based |
|---|---|---|---|
| Chicken breast<br>Chickpeas<br>Hard-boiled eggs<br>Pork tenderloin<br>Salmon<br>Shrimp<br>Flank steak<br>Tempeh | Blue cheese<br>Cheddar<br>Feta<br>Goat cheese<br>Monterey Jack<br>Mozzarella<br>Parmesan | Avocado<br>Almonds<br>Dried apricots<br>Capers<br>Dried cranberries<br>Croutons<br>Olives<br>Salami or ham<br>Sunflower seeds<br>Walnuts | Balsamic vinaigrette<br>Lemon vinaigrette<br>Red wine vinaigrette<br>**Or make your own:** Whisk together 2 Tbsp. vinegar or lemon juice; 1 clove garlic, minced; ¼ tsp. dried thyme; and ⅛ tsp. each salt and black pepper, then whisk in ¼ cup olive oil. Use 2 Tbsp. per salad. |

Roasted Steak and Tomato Salad

## Roasted Steak and Tomato Salad

**16g CARB**

**SERVES** 4
**HANDS ON** 20 min.
**TOTAL** 40 min.

- 2 8-oz. beef shoulder petite tenders or two 8-oz. beef tenderloin steaks, trimmed
- 1 tsp. cracked black pepper
- ¼ tsp. kosher salt
- 6 small tomatoes, halved, or 3 tomatoes, quartered
- 2 tsp. olive oil
- ¼ cup finely shredded Parmesan cheese
- ½ tsp. dried oregano, crushed
- 8 cups torn romaine lettuce
- 1 14-oz. can artichoke hearts, drained and quartered
- ⅓ cup red onion slivers
- 3 Tbsp. balsamic vinegar
- 1 Tbsp. olive oil

**1.** Preheat oven to 400°F. Sprinkle meat with pepper and salt, pressing gently to adhere. Let stand at room temperature 20 minutes.
**2.** Arrange tomato halves, cut sides down, on half of a large rimmed baking sheet. In a large skillet heat the 2 tsp. oil over medium-high. Add meat; cook about 8 minutes or until well browned on all sides. Transfer meat to the other side of the baking sheet.
**3.** Roast 8 to 10 minutes for medium (145°F). Remove meat from oven. Cover with foil and let stand. Move oven rack for broiling.
**4.** Turn oven to broil. Turn tomatoes cut sides up. Combine Parmesan and oregano; sprinkle over tomatoes. Broil 4 to 5 inches from heat about 2 minutes or until cheese is melted and golden.
**5.** In a bowl combine lettuce, artichoke hearts, and onion. Drizzle with vinegar and the 1 Tbsp. oil; toss to coat. Arrange on plates. Slice steak and arrange over lettuce with tomato halves.

**TIP** Beef shoulder petite tenders are lean and flavorful cuts that are a better value than beef tenderloin. They can be hard to find, so ask for them at the meat counter.

**PER SERVING** (2 cups salad + 3 oz. beef + 3 tomato pieces each) **CAL** 299, **FAT** 14 g (4 g sat. fat), **CHOL** 69 mg, **SODIUM** 416 mg, **CARB** 16 g (5 g fiber, 8 g sugars), **PRO** 29 g

Smoky Steak Salad with Arugula and Oranges

## Smoky Steak Salad with Arugula and Oranges

**22g CARB**

**SERVES** 4
**HANDS ON** 30 min.
**TOTAL** 40 min.

- 8 oz. beef flank steak, trimmed
- ½ tsp. kosher salt
- ½ tsp. cracked black pepper
- 3 tsp. olive oil
- 4 navel oranges
- 1½ Tbsp. white wine vinegar
- 1½ tsp. honey
- 1 tsp. Dijon mustard
- 1 clove garlic, minced
- ½ tsp. smoked paprika
- ½ tsp. chopped fresh rosemary
- 1 5-oz. pkg. baby arugula
- ½ cup very thinly sliced red onion
- 1 oz. goat cheese (chèvre) or feta cheese, crumbled (¼ cup)
- ¼ cup chopped pecans, toasted

**1.** Sprinkle both sides of meat with ¼ tsp. of the salt and ¼ tsp. of the pepper. In a medium skillet heat 1 tsp. of the oil over medium-high. Add meat; cook 12 to 16 minutes or until desired doneness (150°F for medium), turning once. Remove from skillet. Let stand 10 minutes before thinly slicing across the grain.
**2.** Meanwhile, remove 1 tsp. zest and squeeze ¼ cup juice from one of the oranges. Peel and slice the remaining oranges. For vinaigrette, in a small bowl whisk together orange zest and juice, the next six ingredients (through rosemary), and the remaining 2 tsp. oil, ¼ tsp. salt, and ¼ tsp. pepper.
**3.** On a large platter arrange steak, orange slices, and arugula. Top arugula with red onion, cheese, and pecans. Drizzle with vinaigrette. If desired, sprinkle with additional pepper.

**PER SERVING** (2½ cups each) **CAL** 280, **FAT** 14 g (4 g sat. fat), **CHOL** 45 mg, **SODIUM** 242 mg, **CARB** 22 g (5 g fiber, 16 g sugars), **PRO** 17 g

Shrimp,
Couscous,
and Melon
Salad

## Shrimp, Couscous, and Melon Salad

**44g CARB**

SERVES 6
TOTAL 30 min.

- ¼ cup olive oil
- ¼ cup lime juice
- ¼ cup lemon juice
- 3 Tbsp. thinly sliced shallot
- ½ tsp. coarse salt
- ½ tsp. black pepper
- 1⅔ cups Israeli (large pearl) couscous
- 1 lb. peeled and deveined cooked large shrimp
- 5 cups cantaloupe chunks
- 3 cups fresh spinach
- 2 cups sliced cucumber
- ¼ cup fresh basil leaves

**1.** For dressing, in a small bowl whisk together the first six ingredients (through pepper) until combined.
**2.** In a medium saucepan cook couscous in boiling salted water 6 to 8 minutes or until tender; drain. Rinse with cold water; drain again.
**3.** On a platter arrange couscous and the remaining ingredients. Drizzle with dressing. Toss before serving.

**PER SERVING** (2⅓ cups each) **CAL** 346, **FAT** 10 g (1 g sat. fat), **CHOL** 122 mg, **SODIUM** 284 mg, **CARB** 44 g (2 g fiber, 12 g sugars), **PRO** 22 g

Grilled Salmon Salad with Raspberry Vinaigrette

## Grilled Salmon Salad with Raspberry Vinaigrette

**21g CARB**

SERVES 4
HANDS ON 30 min.
TOTAL 45 min.

- 4 4-oz. fresh or frozen skinless salmon fillets, 1 inch thick
- 4 cups fresh raspberries
- 3 Tbsp. red wine vinegar
- 1 Tbsp. sugar
- 1 tsp. Dijon mustard
- ½ tsp. salt
- ½ tsp. lemon zest
- ¼ tsp. black pepper
  Nonstick cooking spray
- 6 cups fresh baby spinach
- ½ cup crumbled reduced-fat feta cheese (2 oz.)
- ¼ cup chopped toasted walnuts

**1.** Thaw salmon, if frozen. For vinaigrette, in a small saucepan combine 2 cups of the raspberries, the vinegar, sugar, and mustard. Bring to boiling; reduce heat. Simmer, uncovered, 8 to 10 minutes or until berries have broken down and mixture is slightly thick. Cool slightly. Press through a fine-mesh sieve; discard seeds. Stir in ¼ tsp. of the salt, the lemon zest, and ⅛ tsp. of the pepper. Cool completely. If desired, thin with a little water.
**2.** Lightly coat salmon with cooking spray and sprinkle with the remaining ¼ tsp. salt and ⅛ tsp. pepper. Grease grill rack. Grill salmon, covered, over medium 8 to 12 minutes or just until salmon flakes, turning once.
**3.** In a large bowl combine spinach and vinaigrette; toss to coat. Divide mixture among plates. Top with salmon, the remaining 2 cups raspberries, the cheese, walnuts, and, if desired, additional lemon zest.

**PER SERVING** (2 cups salad + 1 salmon fillet each) **CAL** 325, **FAT** 14 g (3 g sat. fat), **CHOL** 67 mg, **SODIUM** 577 mg, **CARB** 21 g (10 g fiber, 9 g sugars), **PRO** 29 g

Sweet Potato, White Bean Hummus, and Israeli Salad

## Sweet Potato, White Bean Hummus, and Israeli Salad

**43g** CARB | SERVES 4
TOTAL 35 min.

- 1 14- to 16-oz. sweet potato
- 1 cup no-salt-added Great Northern or cannellini beans, rinsed and drained
- ⅓ cup unsalted cashew butter
- ¼ cup water
- 2 tsp. lemon juice
- 2 cloves garlic, minced
- ½ tsp. salt
- ¼ tsp. ground cumin
- ¼ cup finely chopped red onion
- ¼ cup white balsamic vinegar
- ¾ cup chopped yellow bell pepper
- ½ cup chopped tomato
- ½ cup chopped cucumber
- 2 Tbsp. chopped fresh parsley

**1.** Prick potato all over with a fork. Place sweet potato in a microwave-safe dish. Cover with plastic wrap. Microwave 4 to 6 minutes or until tender.
**2.** Meanwhile, for hummus, in a medium bowl combine beans, cashew butter, water, lemon juice, half of the garlic, ¼ tsp. of the salt, and ⅛ tsp. of the cumin. Mash to desired consistency.
**3.** For dressing, in a small screw-top jar combine 1 Tbsp. of the onion, the vinegar, and the remaining garlic, ¼ tsp. salt, and ⅛ tsp. cumin. Cover and shake well.
**4.** In another bowl combine the remaining onion, bell pepper, tomato, cucumber, and parsley. Drizzle with the dressing; toss to combine.
**5.** Cut potato into quarters. Place on plates. Using a fork, loosen sweet potato flesh. Top with hummus and vegetable mixture.

**PER SERVING** (¼ of a sweet potato + ⅓ cup hummus + ½ cup vegetable mixture each) **CAL** 298, **FAT** 11 g (2 g sat. fat), **CHOL** 0 mg, **SODIUM** 452 mg, **CARB** 43 g (6 g fiber, 12 g sugars), **PRO** 9 g

## Mediterranean Lentil and Kale Salad

**17g** CARB | SERVES 4
TOTAL 15 min.

- ¼ cup red wine vinegar
- 2 Tbsp. olive oil
- 1 Tbsp. finely chopped dried tomatoes (not oil-packed)
- 1 clove garlic, minced
- ½ tsp. Dijon mustard
- ¼ tsp. salt
- ¼ tsp. black pepper
- 1 5-oz. pkg. fresh baby kale (8 cups)
- 1 9-oz. pkg. refrigerated steamed lentils, such as Melissa's
- 1 cup chopped red bell pepper
- ¼ cup shredded Parmesan cheese (1 oz.)

**1.** For vinaigrette, in a large serving bowl whisk together the first seven ingredients (through black pepper). Add kale; toss to coat. Top with lentils and sweet pepper. Sprinkle with cheese.

**TIP** To cook your own lentils, rinse and drain ¾ cup dried brown, French, or yellow lentils. In a medium saucepan bring 2 cups water to boiling. Stir in lentils. Return to boiling; reduce heat. Cover and simmer 20 to 25 minutes or just until tender. Drain and cool. Store in the refrigerator up to 3 days. Makes 1¾ cups.

**PER SERVING** (2½ cups each) **CAL** 179, **FAT** 9 g (2 g sat. fat), **CHOL** 4 mg, **SODIUM** 439 mg, **CARB** 17 g (7 g fiber, 3 g sugars), **PRO** 9 g

Mediterranean
Lentil and
Kale Salad

Fresh
Taco
Salad

## Fresh Taco Salad

**29g**
**CARB**

**SERVES** 6
**TOTAL** 30 min.

- 4 cups mixed salad greens
- 1 15-oz. can black beans, rinsed and drained
- 2 ears corn, husks and silks removed and kernels cut off the cobs
- ¾ cup matchstick-size pieces peeled jicama
- ½ cup chopped tomato
- 1 medium avocado, halved, seeded, peeled, and sliced
- 1 fresh jalapeño pepper, stemmed, seeded, and thinly sliced (tip, p. 154)
- 2 cups multigrain tortilla chips with flaxseeds
- ½ cup refrigerated fresh salsa
- ½ cup crumbled queso fresco (2 oz.)
- 1 recipe Cilantro Ranch Dressing

**1.** Line a large platter with salad greens. In a medium bowl combine the next four ingredients (through tomato). Spoon over greens. Arrange avocado and jalapeño slices over top. Top with chips, salsa, and cheese. Drizzle with Cilantro Ranch Dressing.

**TIP** If fresh corn isn't in season, use 1 cup frozen whole kernel corn, thawed.

**CILANTRO RANCH DRESSING** In a bowl whisk together ⅓ cup light sour cream; ¼ cup buttermilk; 2 Tbsp. chopped fresh cilantro; 1 Tbsp. each chopped fresh chives and lime juice; 2 cloves garlic, minced; and 1 tsp. chili powder.

**PER SERVING** (2¼ cups each) **CAL** 214, **FAT** 9 g (3 g sat. fat), **CHOL** 11 mg, **SODIUM** 447 mg, **CARB** 29 g (8 g fiber, 4 g sugars), **PRO** 10 g

Poached Egg and Veggie Salad

## Poached Egg and Veggie Salad

**16g**
**CARB**

**SERVES** 4
**TOTAL** 30 min.

- 4 cups water
- 1 Tbsp. cider vinegar
- 4 eggs
- 2 tsp. olive oil
- 3 cups sliced fresh mushrooms
- 5 cups chopped fresh kale or spinach
- 2 cups grape tomatoes, quartered
- ¼ tsp. sea salt
- ¼ tsp. black pepper
- ¼ cup sliced red onion (optional)

**1.** In an extra-large skillet bring the water and vinegar to simmering. Break an egg into a custard cup and slip egg into simmering water. Repeat with remaining eggs, allowing each egg an equal amount of space. Simmer 3 to 5 minutes or until whites are completely set and yolks begin to thicken but are not hard. Remove eggs with a slotted spoon and keep warm.

**2.** Discard liquid in skillet and wipe skillet dry. Add oil to skillet and heat over medium. Add mushrooms; cook 3 to 5 minutes or until tender, stirring occasionally. Add kale; cook about 30 seconds or until wilted, stirring frequently. Stir in tomatoes, salt, and pepper; heat through.

**3.** Spoon vegetable mixture into four bowls. Top each with a poached egg and, if desired, red onion and additional pepper.

**PER SERVING** (¾ cup vegetable mixture + 1 poached egg each) **CAL** 179, **FAT** 8 g (2 g sat. fat), **CHOL** 186 mg, **SODIUM** 417 mg, **CARB** 16 g (5 g fiber, 8 g sugars), **PRO** 13 g

# 3 COMFORTING SOUPS & STEWS

People love soup suppers because they're one-pot bowls of comfort. As a bonus, we curbed the sodium and loaded them with lean protein and colorful produce. Go simple with no-watch Beef Oven Stew or go global with Spanish-Style Gigante Bean Soup with chubby butter beans.

54

57

65

### Pesto Chicken-Quinoa Stew

**15g**
**CARB**

**SERVES** 4
**TOTAL** 15 min.

2 cups chopped fresh kale or spinach
1 14.5-oz. can reduced-sodium chicken broth
1⅓ cups shredded rotisserie chicken breast
1 cup cooked quinoa
2 Tbsp. chopped roasted red bell pepper
2 tsp. basil pesto
½ tsp. lemon zest
¼ tsp. kosher salt
¼ tsp. black pepper

**1.** In a large saucepan combine all ingredients. Bring to a simmer over medium, stirring occasionally.

**FOR INDIVIDUAL SERVINGS** Divide all of the ingredients among four 2- to 3-cup containers. Store in refrigerator up to 4 days. To serve, microwave one portion at a time 1½ to 2 minutes or until heated through, stirring once.

**PER SERVING** *(1 cup each)* **CAL** 190, **FAT** 8 g *(2 g sat. fat)*, **CHOL** 29 mg, **SODIUM** 441 mg, **CARB** 15 g *(3 g fiber, 1 g sugars)*, **PRO** 15 g

## Lemon Chicken and Wild Rice Soup

**34g CARB**

SERVES 4
HANDS ON 20 min.
TOTAL 1 hr. 5 min.

- 1 Tbsp. olive oil
- 1 cup chopped onion
- 1 cup sliced carrots
- 1 cup sliced celery
- 6 cloves garlic, minced
- 5 cups reduced-sodium chicken broth
- ¾ cup wild rice, rinsed and drained
- ½ tsp. salt
- ½ tsp. black pepper
- 2 cups shredded cooked chicken breast
- ¼ cup chopped fresh dill
- 1 tsp. lemon zest
- ¼ cup lemon juice

**1.** In a 5- to 6-qt. Dutch oven heat oil over medium. Add onion, celery, carrots, and garlic. Cook 8 to 10 minutes or until tender, stirring occasionally. Add broth, rice, salt, and pepper. Bring to boiling; reduce heat. Cover and simmer 40 to 45 minutes or until rice is tender, stirring occasionally. Stir in the remaining ingredients; heat through.

**PER SERVING** *(2 cups each)* **CAL.** 299, **FAT** 6 g *(1 g sat. fat)*, **CHOL** 54 mg, **SODIUM** 469 mg, **CARB** 34 g *(4 g fiber, 5 g sugars)*, **PRO** 28 g.

Chicken
and
Vegetable
Soup with
Pasta

## Chicken and Vegetable Soup with Pasta

**29g CARB**

SERVES 4
HANDS ON 25 min.
TOTAL 40 min.

- 1 Tbsp. olive oil
- ½ cup chopped onion
- ½ cup chopped carrot
- ½ cup chopped red bell pepper
- 1 clove garlic, minced
- 4 cups reduced-sodium chicken broth
- 2 cups chopped cooked chicken (10 oz.)
- 2 cups cooked pasta (such as campanelle or gemelli)
- 4 cups fresh baby spinach
- 2 Tbsp. chopped fresh flat-leaf parsley
- ¼ tsp. salt
  Black pepper

**1.** In a large saucepan heat oil over medium. Add the next four ingredients (through garlic); cook 5 minutes, stirring frequently. Add broth and chicken. Bring to boiling; reduce heat. Cover and simmer 5 to 10 minutes or until vegetables are tender.

**2.** Add the cooked pasta; heat through. Stir in spinach and parsley; cook 1 to 2 minutes more or just until wilted. Stir in salt and the black pepper to taste.

**PER SERVING** *(1¾ cups each)* **CAL** 320, **FAT** 9 g *(2 g sat. fat)*, **CHOL** 62 mg, **SODIUM** 672 mg, **CARB** 29 g *(3 g fiber, 4 g sugars)*, **PRO** 29 g

Harvest
Chicken
Lentil
Chili

## Harvest Chicken Lentil Chili

**24g CARB**

SERVES 8
HANDS ON 30 min.
TOTAL 1 hr. 30 min.

- 1 Tbsp. olive oil
- 2 cups coarsely chopped onions
- 1 cup coarsely chopped carrots
- 1 cup chopped celery
- 2 lb. bone-in chicken thighs, skin removed
- 4 cups reduced-sodium chicken broth
- 1 cup water
- ¾ cup dried brown lentils, rinsed and drained
- 1 15-oz. can pumpkin
- 1 14.5-oz. can no-salt-added diced tomatoes, undrained
- 1 Tbsp. chili powder
- 1 tsp. ground cumin
- 1 tsp. dried oregano, crushed
- 1 to 2 Tbsp. bottled Louisiana hot sauce
  Plain fat-free Greek yogurt and/or roasted pumpkin seeds (peptitas) (optional)

**1.** In a 4-qt. Dutch oven heat oil over medium-high. Add onions, carrots, and celery. Cook 6 to 8 minutes or until onions are tender, stirring occasionally. Add chicken, broth, and the water. Bring to boiling; reduce heat. Cover and simmer about 20 minutes or until chicken is done (at least 175°F). Remove chicken from Dutch oven; cool slightly. Remove chicken from bones and chop chicken; discard bones.
**2.** Meanwhile, stir lentils into broth mixture. Return to boiling; reduce heat. Cover and simmer about 30 minutes or until lentils are tender.
**3.** Stir in chicken and the next five ingredients (through oregano); cover and heat through. Stir in hot sauce.
**4.** If desired, top servings with yogurt, pumpkin seeds, and/or additional chili powder.

**PER SERVING** (1 ½ cups each) **CAL** 223, **FAT** 5 g (1 g sat. fat), **CHOL** 64 mg, **SODIUM** 506 mg, **CARB** 24 g (10 g fiber, 7 g sugars), **PRO** 22 g

Beefy
French Onion
Noodle Soup

## Beefy French Onion Noodle Soup

**24g CARB** | SERVES 6
TOTAL 1 hr.

- ¼ cup vegetable oil
- 2 cups sliced fresh mushrooms
- 3 cups thinly sliced onions
- 10 oz. boneless beef sirloin steak, trimmed and cut into very thin strips
- ¼ tsp. salt
  Black pepper
- 2 32-oz. boxes 50%-less-sodium beef broth
- ⅓ cup dry white wine (optional)
- 1 Tbsp. Worcestershire sauce
- 4 oz. very wide home-style egg noodles, broken if long
- 6 slices French bread, toasted (optional)
- ¾ cup shredded Swiss, Gruyère, or Jarlsberg cheese (3 oz.) (optional)

**1.** In a 5- to 6-qt. Dutch oven heat 1 Tbsp. of the oil over medium-high. Add mushrooms and cook until softened. Add onion and an additional 1 Tbsp. oil; cook and stir over medium until mushrooms and onions are lightly browned. Reduce heat to low. Cook, covered, about 10 minutes or until golden, stirring if necessary. Remove from pan.
**2.** Sprinkle beef strips with salt and pepper to taste. In the Dutch oven heat the remaining 2 Tbsp. oil over medium-high. Add beef; cook and stir until browned. Remove beef from pan. Stir in beef broth, wine (if using), Worcestershire sauce, and ¼ tsp. pepper. Bring to boiling; add noodles and onion mixture. Cook, uncovered, according to noodle package instructions; return meat to Dutch oven the last 3 minutes of cooking.
**3.** Meanwhile, if desired, preheat broiler. Arrange toasted bread on a baking sheet and sprinkle with cheese. Broil 3 to 4 inches from the heat about 1 minute or until cheese melts and turns light brown. Top each serving of soup with a toasted bread slice.

**PER SERVING** *(1⅓ cups each)* **CAL** 275, **FAT** 12 g *(2 g sat. fat)*, **CHOL** 44 mg, **SODIUM** 664 mg, **CARB** 24 g *(2 g fiber, 6 g sugars)*, **PRO** 18 g

Beef Oven Stew

## Beef Oven Stew

**37g CARB** | SERVES 6
HANDS ON 15 min.
TOTAL 2 hr. 15 min.

- 4 medium red-skin potatoes, cut into 1-inch pieces
- 4 medium carrots, cut into 1-inch pieces
- 1 cup coarsely chopped onion
- ½ cup sliced celery
- ½ cup water or 50%-less-sodium beef broth
- 2 Tbsp. quick-cooking tapioca
- 1 lb. beef stew meat, trimmed and cut into 1-inch pieces
- 2 14.5-oz. cans no-salt-added diced tomatoes, undrained
- 1 Tbsp. sugar
- 1 Tbsp. dried Italian seasoning, crushed (optional)
- ½ tsp. salt
- ½ tsp. black pepper

**1.** Preheat oven to 325°F. In a 3-qt. rectangular baking dish combine the first five ingredients (through water). Sprinkle vegetables with tapioca. Add meat. In a medium bowl combine the remaining ingredients; pour over meat.
**2.** Bake, covered, about 2 hours or until meat is tender. Stir before serving.

**TIP** Save a few dollars and use 1-inch pieces of boneless pork shoulder roast instead of beef stew meat in this oven-to-table stew.

**PER SERVING** *(1¾ cups each)* **CAL** 254, **FAT** 4 g *(1 g sat. fat)*, **CHOL** 48 mg, **SODIUM** 366 mg, **CARB** 37 g *(6 g fiber, 11 g sugars)*, **PRO** 21 g

**Persian-Style Stew**

## Persian-Style Stew

**53g**
**CARB**

**SERVES** 6
**HANDS ON** 25 min.
**SLOW COOK** 8 hr. 10 min.

- 1 Tbsp. vegetable oil
- 1½ to 2 lb. lamb or beef stew meat, cut into 1-inch cubes
- 3 medium leeks, trimmed, halved, rinsed, and cut into 1-inch pieces
- 1 cup chopped onion
- ⅔ cup dried yellow or green split peas, rinsed and drained
- 2 bay leaves
- 4 cloves garlic, sliced
- 1½ tsp. ground cumin
- ¼ tsp. black pepper
- 1 Tbsp. chopped fresh oregano or 1 tsp. dried oregano, crushed
- 3 cups reduced-sodium chicken broth
- ⅓ cup raisins
- 2 Tbsp. lemon juice
- 3 cups hot cooked rice or bulgur
  Lemon wedges

**1.** In a large skillet heat oil over medium-high. Add half of the meat and cook until browned. Remove meat from skillet. Repeat with the remaining meat.
**2.** Place meat in a 3½- or 4-qt. slow cooker. Stir in the next seven ingredients (through pepper) and the dried oregano (if using). Pour broth over all in cooker.
**3.** Cover and cook on low 8 to 10 hours or on high 4 to 5 hours. Turn off cooker. Stir in raisins; cover and let stand 10 minutes. Discard bay leaves. Stir in lemon juice and, if using, fresh oregano.
**4.** Serve stew with rice, lemon wedges, and additional fresh oregano.

**PER SERVING** *(1 cup each)* **CAL** 535, **FAT** 22 g *(10 g sat. fat)*, **CHOL** 75 mg, **SODIUM** 377 mg, **CARB** 53 g *(7 g fiber, 10 g sugars)*, **PRO** 31 g

## Southwest BBQ Pork and Squash Stew

**27g**
**CARB**

**SERVES** 8
**HANDS ON** 25 min.
**SLOW COOK** 8 hr.

- 1½ lb. pork tenderloin, cut into 1-inch cubes
- 2 Tbsp. vegetable oil
- 1 medium onion, cut into ¼-inch-thick wedges
- 2½ cups reduced-sodium chicken broth
- ½ cup barbecue sauce
- 1 2-lb. butternut squash, peeled and cut into 1-inch cubes (6 cups)
- 2 medium carrots, cut into ½-inch pieces
- 1 poblano pepper, seeded and cut into 1-inch pieces (tip, p. 154)
- 1 14.5-oz. can diced tomatoes with mild green chiles, undrained
- 1 Tbsp. chili powder
  Corn bread or corn muffins (optional)

**1.** In a large skillet heat oil over medium-high. Add half of the meat and cook until browned. Transfer meat to a 6-qt. slow cooker. Repeat with remaining meat. Stir in the next eight ingredients (through chili powder).
**2.** Cover and cook on low 8 to 10 hours or on high 4 to 5 hours. If desired, serve with corn bread.

**PER SERVING** *(1⅓ cups each)* **CAL** 241, **FAT** 6 g *(1 g sat. fat)*, **CHOL** 55 mg, **SODIUM** 576 mg, **CARB** 27 g *(4 g fiber, 12 g sugars)*, **PRO** 22 g

Southwest
BBQ
Pork and
Squash
Stew

## QUICK TIP

Look for fresh cubed butternut squash in the produce section of your supermarket to save time peeling and cutting.

Pork
Meatball
and Escarole
Soup

## Pork Meatball and Escarole Soup

**5g CARB**

SERVES 6
HANDS ON 35 min.
TOTAL 45 min.

- 1 egg
- ⅓ cup very finely chopped fresh button mushrooms
- ¼ tsp. freshly grated nutmeg
- ⅛ tsp. salt
- ⅛ tsp. black pepper
- 1 lb. ground pork
- ¼ cup finely chopped fresh flat-leaf parsley
- ¼ cup finely grated Parmesan cheese (optional)
- 2 Tbsp. olive oil
- 1 cup thinly sliced celery
- ½ cup coarsely chopped onion
- 1 head escarole, leaves torn into large pieces (7 cups)
- 4 cups reduced-sodium chicken broth
- 2 cups water
- ½ cup flat-leaf parsley leaves

1. For meatballs, in a bowl whisk together the first five ingredients (through pepper). Stir in pork, the ¼ cup chopped parsley, and, if desired, Parmesan.
2. In a 5- to 6-qt. pot heat oil over medium-high. Add celery and onion;

cook and stir about 5 minutes or until tender. Add escarole, broth, the water, and the ½ cup parsley leaves. Bring to boiling; reduce heat to maintain a simmer.
3. Drop rounded tablespoons of pork mixture into broth. Gently stir meatballs in broth. Simmer, covered, about 10 minutes or until meatballs are no longer pink (160°F). If desired, serve with additional Parmesan cheese and pepper.

**PER SERVING** *(1 ½ cups each)* **CAL** 249, **FAT** 18 g *(5 g sat. fat)*, **CHOL** 82 mg, **SODIUM** 505 mg, **CARB** 5 g *(2 g fiber, 1 g sugars)*, **PRO** 18 g

---

## Mediterranean Fisherman's Stew with Roasted Garlic Crostini

**23g CARB**

SERVES 6
HANDS ON 30 min.
TOTAL 1 hr. 15 min.

- 1 bulb garlic
- 1 tsp. olive oil
- 2 lb. fresh or frozen skinless cod fillets
- 12 oz. fresh or frozen large shrimp in shells
- 12 oz. fresh mussels in shells
- 3 Tbsp. olive oil

- 1 Tbsp. finely chopped fresh parsley
- 5 cloves garlic, minced
- 1 Tbsp. no-salt-added tomato paste
- 1 cup dry white wine
- 2 cups chopped tomatoes
- ½ to 1 tsp. crushed red pepper
- ¼ tsp. black pepper
- 1 cup water
- 6 1-oz. slices whole wheat Italian or sourdough bread

1. Preheat oven to 400°F. Cut off top ½ inch of garlic bulb to expose ends of individual cloves. Leaving bulb whole, remove any loose, papery outer layers. Place bulb, cut end up, on a double-thick piece of foil. Drizzle bulb with the 1 tsp. oil. Bring foil up around bulb and fold edges together to loosely enclose. Roast 50 to 60 minutes or until tender; cool.
2. Meanwhile, thaw fish and shrimp, if frozen. Peel and devein shrimp, leaving tails intact if desired. Cut fish into 2-inch pieces. Scrub mussels under cold running water. Using your fingers, pull out beards that are visible between the shells.
3. In a 6-qt. Dutch oven heat 2 Tbsp. of the oil over medium. Add parsley and minced garlic; cook and stir 30 seconds. Add tomato paste; cook and stir 1 minute more. Add wine; increase heat to high. Cook about 5 minutes or until wine is evaporated, stirring frequently. Add tomatoes, crushed red pepper, and black pepper. Cook about 5 minutes or until tomatoes are softened, stirring occasionally. Stir in the water. Cover and simmer 10 minutes.
4. Layer fish, shrimp, and mussels on tomato mixture. Cover and cook, without stirring, 5 to 7 minutes or until fish flakes easily, shrimp are opaque, and mussel shells open. Discard any mussels that do not open.
5. For garlic crostini, brush both sides of bread with the remaining 1 Tbsp. oil. Place bread on a baking sheet. Bake 3 to 5 minutes or until toasted. Squeeze garlic bulb from bottom of papery husk so cloves pop out. Spread roasted garlic over toast.
6. If desired, sprinkle servings with additional parsley. Serve with garlic crostini.

**PER SERVING** *(2 cups each)* **CAL** 417, **FAT** 12 g *(2 g sat. fat)*, **CHOL** 160 mg, **SODIUM** 410 mg, **CARB** 23 g *(3 g fiber, 3 g sugars)*, **PRO** 47 g

Mediterranean
Fisherman's
Stew with Roasted
Garlic Crostini

Curried
Chickpea
Stew

## Thai Peanut Squash Soup

**21g**
**CARB**

| SERVES 6 |
| TOTAL 15 min. |

- 2 tsp. olive oil
- ½ cup finely chopped onion
- 2 Tbsp. red curry paste
- 1 Tbsp. grated fresh ginger
- 2 cloves garlic, minced
- 2 10-oz. pkg. frozen cubed butternut squash, thawed
- 1 13.5-oz. can unsweetened light coconut milk
- ¾ cup reduced-sodium chicken or vegetable broth
- ¼ cup natural peanut butter
- 2 Tbsp. lime juice
- ½ tsp. kosher salt
   Plain yogurt, chopped fresh cilantro, and/or sriracha sauce (optional)

**1.** In a large saucepan heat oil over medium-high. Add onion; cook 2 minutes, stirring frequently. Stir in curry paste, ginger, and garlic; cook and stir 30 seconds more. Stir in squash, coconut milk, and broth.
**2.** Bring to boiling; reduce heat. Simmer 5 minutes. Reduce heat to low. Stir in peanut butter, lime juice, and salt.
**3.** Using an immersion blender, carefully blend soup until smooth. (Or cool soup slightly and transfer to a blender. Cover and blend until smooth.) If desired, top servings with yogurt, cilantro, and/or sriracha sauce.

**PER SERVING** (1 cup each) **CAL** 190, **FAT** 11 g (4 g sat. fat), **CHOL** 0 mg, **SODIUM** 269 mg, **CARB** 21 g (3 g fiber, 5 g sugars), **PRO** 6 g

## Curried Chickpea Stew

**39g**
**CARB**

| SERVES 8 |
| HANDS ON 30 min. |
| TOTAL 55 min. |

- 1 10-oz. bag spinach or other sturdy greens
- 1½ Tbsp. canola oil
- 1 cup chopped onion
- 1 2-inch piece fresh ginger, peeled and minced
- ½ to 1 small jalapeño pepper, seeded and finely chopped (tip, p. 154)
- 3 cloves garlic, minced
- 1 Tbsp. curry powder
- 1½ cups thinly sliced carrots
- 3 cups bite-size cauliflower florets
- 2 15-oz. cans reduced-sodium chickpeas, rinsed and drained
- 2 14.5-oz. cans no-salt-added diced tomatoes, drained
- ½ cup fat-free half-and-half
- ⅓ cup canned unsweetened light coconut milk

**1.** Place spinach and 1 Tbsp. water in a microwave-safe dish; cover. Microwave 1 to 2 minutes or until just wilted, stirring occasionally. Transfer to a colander; let drain. When cool enough to handle, squeeze out any excess water. Coarsely chop.
**2.** In a large nonstick skillet with high sides or a Dutch oven heat oil over medium. Add onion; cook about 8 minutes or until translucent, stirring occasionally. Add ginger, jalapeño, garlic, and curry powder; cook and stir 30 seconds. Add carrots and 2 Tbsp. water; cover and cook about 10 minutes or until carrots are tender, stirring occasionally and adding more water if the mixture becomes dry. Add cauliflower; cover and cook 5 to 10 minutes more or until just tender-crisp, stirring occasionally.
**3.** Stir in the remaining ingredients. Bring to a simmer; reduce heat. Simmer, uncovered, 15 minutes, stirring occasionally. Stir in spinach; heat through.

**TO MAKE AHEAD** Transfer cooled soup to an airtight container. Refrigerate up to 3 days or freeze up to 1 month.

**PER SERVING** (1¼ cups each) **CAL** 249, **FAT** 7 g (1 g sat. fat), **CHOL** 1 mg, **SODIUM** 309 mg, **CARB** 39 g (10 g fiber, 7 g sugars), **PRO** 11 g

Thai Peanut Squash Soup

## QUICK TIP

Using frozen squash allows this hearty soup to be ready in just 15 minutes. If you want to use fresh squash, steam 4 cups peeled and cubed squash until tender. Use in place of the two frozen packages.

## Hearty Turkey and Chickpea Stew

**41g CARB**

**SERVES** 4
**HANDS ON** 20 min.
**TOTAL** 30 min.

- **2** 15-oz. cans reduced-sodium chickpeas, rinsed and drained
- **1** Tbsp. olive oil
- **12** oz. 93%-lean ground turkey
- **½** tsp. dried oregano
- **½** tsp. fennel seeds, crushed
- **½** tsp. crushed red pepper
- **1** cup chopped onion
- **¾** cup chopped carrots
- **4** cloves garlic, minced, or ½ tsp. garlic powder
- **3** Tbsp. tomato paste
- **1** 32-oz. carton reduced-sodium chicken broth (4 cups)
- **¼** tsp. black pepper
- **⅛** tsp. salt
- **3** cups IQF (individually quick-frozen) spinach (8 oz.)
- **¼** cup grated Parmesan cheese (optional)

**1.** Mash one can of the chickpeas with a potato masher or fork.
**2.** In a large pot heat oil over medium-high. Add turkey, oregano, fennel seeds, and crushed red pepper; cook and stir 2 to 3 minutes or until the turkey is no longer pink. Add onion, carrots, and garlic; cook 3 to 4 minutes or until softened, stirring often. Add tomato paste; cook and stir 30 seconds.
**3.** Stir in broth, the mashed and whole chickpeas, black pepper, and salt. Bring to a simmer; reduce heat to medium. Cover and cook at a brisk simmer about 10 minutes or until the vegetables are tender and the flavors have blended.
**4.** Stir in spinach; increase heat to medium-high. Cook and stir 1 to 2 minutes or until heated through. If desired, top servings with Parmesan.

**PER SERVING** *(2 cups each)* **CAL** 401, **FAT** 13 g *(2 g sat. fat)*, **CHOL** 49 mg, **SODIUM** 643 mg, **CARB** 41 g *(13 g fiber, 10 g sugars)*, **PRO** 32 g

Spanish-Style Gigante Bean Soup

## Spanish-Style Gigante Bean Soup

**42g CARB**

**SERVES** 8
**HANDS ON** 30 min.
**TOTAL** 3 hr. 15 min.

- 1 lb. dried gigante or large butter beans (lima beans)
- 2 Tbsp. olive oil
- ½ cup finely chopped onion
- 6 cloves garlic, minced
- 2 pints grape tomatoes
- 1 cup bottled roasted red bell peppers, chopped
- 2 tsp. smoked paprika
- ½ tsp. saffron threads, crushed, or ½ tsp. ground turmeric
- 2 bay leaves
- 2 cups vegetable broth or reduced-sodium chicken broth
- ½ tsp. salt
- 1 recipe Parsley Topper (optional)

1. Rinse beans. In a 6-qt. pot combine beans and 8 cups water. Bring to boiling; reduce heat. Cover and simmer 2 minutes. Remove from heat. Let stand, covered, 1 hour. (Or place beans and water in pot. Cover and let soak in the refrigerator overnight.) Drain beans; rinse and return to pot. Add 8 cups fresh water. Cover and bring to boiling; reduce heat. Simmer, covered, about 45 minutes or until beans are tender, stirring occasionally. Drain all but 2 cups of the cooking liquid from beans.

2. Rinse the pot. Heat oil in the pot over medium. Add onion and garlic; cook 3 to 4 minutes or until tender. Add the next five ingredients (through bay leaves). Stir in ½ cup of the reserved cooking liquid. Bring to boiling; reduce heat to medium-low. Simmer, uncovered, about 15 minutes or until tomatoes start to split, stirring occasionally. Stir in broth, salt, beans, and the remaining 1½ cups cooking liquid. Bring to boiling; reduce heat. Cover and simmer 45 minutes. Discard bay leaves. If desired, top servings with Parsley Topper.

**TIP** To save time, use four 16-oz. cans butter beans, rinsed and drained, instead of the dried beans. Skip Step 1. Add beans as directed in Step 2. Substitute 2 cups fresh water for the cooking liquid.

**PER SERVING** (1⅓ cups each) **CAL** 257, **FAT** , 4 g, (1 g sat. fat), **CHOL** 0 mg, **SODIUM** 437 mg, **CARB** 42 g (12 g fiber, 8 g sugars), **PRO** 13 g

# 4 SMART SANDWICHES

Skip the deli! Make your own sandwiches stuffed with healthy choices built on lower-carb breads and wraps. Check out the stacked Salmon Burgers with Quick Pickled Cucumbers and a perennial favorite, easy Ground Beef Gyros. Add a simple salad or cooked vegetable and your meal is complete.

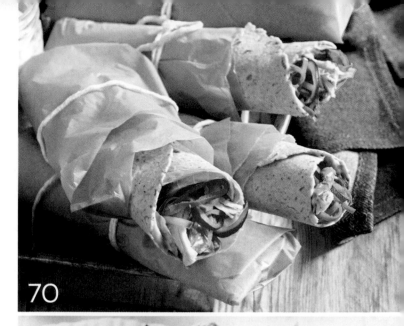

70

76

80

## Chicken and Cucumber Lettuce Cups

**44g CARB** | **SERVES** 4
| **TOTAL** 40 min.

- ¼ cup creamy peanut butter
- 2 Tbsp. reduced-sodium soy sauce
- 2 Tbsp. honey
- 2 Tbsp. water
- 2 tsp. toasted sesame oil
- 2 tsp. olive oil
- 3 green onions, sliced, white and green parts separated
- 2 tsp. finely chopped serrano pepper (tip, *p. 154*)
- 1 Tbsp. grated fresh ginger
- 3 cloves garlic, minced
- 1 lb. uncooked ground chicken breast
- 1 cup finely chopped jicama
- 16 butterhead (Boston or Bibb) lettuce leaves
- 1 cup cooked brown rice
- 1 cup halved and thinly sliced English cucumber
- ½ cup fresh cilantro leaves
  Lime wedges

**1.** For peanut sauce, in a small bowl whisk together the first five ingredients (through sesame oil).

**2.** In a large nonstick skillet heat olive oil over medium. Add green onion whites, serrano pepper, ginger, and garlic; cook about 2 minutes or until starting to soften. Add chicken; cook 3 to 4 minutes or until no longer pink, stirring frequently.

**3.** Add peanut sauce to the skillet; cook about 3 minutes or until sauce has thickened. Remove from heat. Stir in jicama and green onion greens.

**4.** For lettuce cups, make eight stacks of two lettuce leaves each. Divide rice, chicken mixture, cucumber, and cilantro among the lettuce cups. Serve with lime wedges.

**PER SERVING** *(2 cups each)* **CAL** 521, **FAT** 26 g *(3 g sat. fat)*, **CHOL** 54 mg, **SODIUM** 485 mg, **CARB** 44 g *(11 g fiber, 18 g sugars)*, **PRO** 34 g

Greek
Chicken and
Cucumber
Pita
Sandwiches

**TO MAKE AHEAD**

Prepare the yogurt sauce as directed in Step 2. Cover and refrigerate up to 2 days.

## Greek Chicken and Cucumber Pita Sandwiches

**33g CARB**

SERVES 4
HANDS ON 45 min.
TOTAL 1 hr. 45 min.

- 1 **lemon**
- 5 **tsp. olive oil**
- 1 **Tbsp. chopped fresh oregano or 1 tsp. dried oregano, crushed**
- 3 **cloves garlic, chopped**
- ¼ **tsp. crushed red pepper**
- 1 **lb. chicken breast tenders**
- 1 **English cucumber, halved, seeded, and grated + ½ of an English cucumber, halved and sliced**
- ½ **tsp. salt**
- ¾ **cup plain fat-free Greek yogurt**
- 2 **tsp. chopped fresh mint**
- 2 **tsp. chopped fresh dill**
- 1 **tsp. black pepper**
- 2 **6-inch whole wheat pita bread rounds, halved crosswise**
- 4 **lettuce leaves**
- ½ **cup sliced red onion**
- 1 **cup chopped roma tomatoes**

**1.** Remove 1 tsp. zest and squeeze 2 Tbsp. juice from lemon. In a large bowl combine zest, juice, 3 tsp. of the oil, the oregano, two cloves of the garlic, and the crushed red pepper. Add chicken and toss to coat. Marinate in the refrigerator 1 to 4 hours, turning chicken occasionally.

**2.** In a fine-mesh sieve toss grated cucumber with ¼ tsp. of the salt. Let drain 15 minutes; squeeze to release more liquid. Transfer to a medium bowl. Stir in yogurt, mint, dill, black pepper, and the remaining 2 tsp. oil, one clove garlic, and ¼ tsp. salt. Cover and refrigerate until ready to serve.

**3.** Oil the grill rack. Grill chicken, covered, over medium-high 3 to 4 minutes or until done (165°F), turning once.

**4.** Spread the yogurt sauce inside pita halves. Add chicken, lettuce, red onion, tomatoes, and sliced cucumber.

**PER SERVING** (1 sandwich each) **CAL** 353, **FAT** 9 g (1 g sat. fat), **CHOL** 58 mg, **SODIUM** 559 mg, **CARB** 33 g (6 g fiber, 6 g sugars), **PRO** 37 g

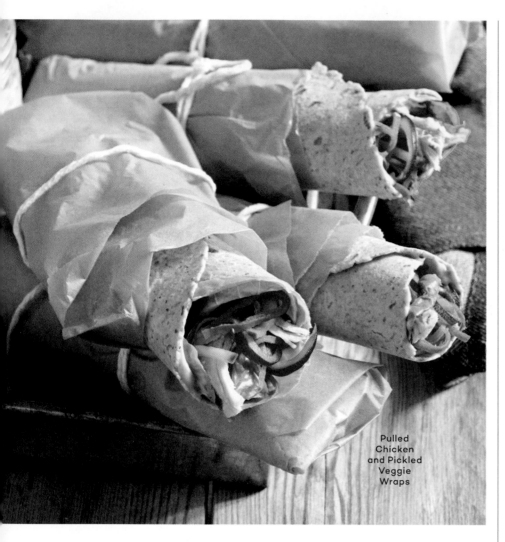

Pulled Chicken and Pickled Veggie Wraps

## Open-Face Chicken Sandwiches with Avocado Slaw

**38g CARB** | **SERVES** 4
**TOTAL** 40 min.

- 1 small clove garlic
- ½ tsp. salt
- 1 avocado, halved, seeded, and peeled
- 2 Tbsp. lemon juice
- 1 Tbsp. olive oil
- 4 cups shredded cabbage with carrot (coleslaw mix)
- ¼ cup unsalted roasted sunflower kernels
- 2 boneless, skinless chicken breast halves (1 lb. total)
- ¾ tsp. black pepper
- 4 tsp. olive oil
- 2 medium tomatoes, chopped
- 2 cloves garlic, minced
- ½ tsp. dried oregano
- 4 slices toasted whole wheat bread

**1.** For slaw, mince the small clove garlic on a cutting board and sprinkle with ¼ tsp. of the salt. Use the broad side of a knife (or a fork) to press and smear the garlic and salt until it makes a paste.

**2.** Transfer the garlic paste to a medium bowl. Add half of the avocado, the lemon juice, and the 1 Tbsp. oil; mash until mostly smooth, leaving some chunks. Add coleslaw mix and sunflower kernels; toss to coat. Chop the remaining avocado; gently stir in.

**3.** Cut each chicken breast half in half horizontally to form two thin cutlets. Sprinkle both sides of cutlets with pepper. In a large nonstick skillet heat 2 tsp. oil over medium-high. Add the cutlets; cook 6 to 8 minutes or until no longer pink in the center, turning once. Transfer to a plate; cover and keep warm.

**4.** In the same pan heat the remaining 2 tsp. oil over medium-high. Add tomatoes, garlic, oregano, and salt; cook and stir about 5 minutes or until the tomatoes and garlic are softened but not mushy. Remove from heat.

**5.** Top bread slices with chicken cutlets and tomato mixture. Serve with avocado slaw.

**PER SERVING** (1 sandwich + about ¾ cup slaw each) **CAL** 502, **FAT** 24 g (4 g sat. fat), **CHOL** 63 mg, **SODIUM** 627 mg, **CARB** 38 g (10 g fiber, 7 g sugars), **PRO** 34 g

## Pulled Chicken and Pickled Veggie Wraps

**27g CARB** | **SERVES** 8
**HANDS ON** 30 min.
**TOTAL** 1 hr. 30 min.

- 2 cups matchstick-cut or coarsely shredded carrots
- 1 cup thin bite-size strips radishes
- 1 cup thinly sliced red onion
- ½ cup rice vinegar
- 2 Tbsp. sugar
- 1 tsp. salt
- ½ cup light mayonnaise
- 1 tsp. sriracha sauce
- 8 7- to 8-inch low-carb whole wheat tortillas, such as La Tortilla Factory
- 8 butterhead (Boston or Bibb) and/or red leaf lettuce leaves
- 2⅔ cups shredded cooked chicken breast

**1.** For pickled vegetables, in a resealable plastic bag combine the first six ingredients (through salt). Seal bag; turn to coat vegetables. Set bag in a shallow dish. Marinate in refrigerator 1 hour. Drain and discard marinade.

**2.** In a small bowl stir together mayonnaise and sriracha sauce.

**3.** Spread mayonnaise mixture over tortillas. Top with lettuce, chicken, and pickled vegetables; roll up tortillas. If desired, drizzle with additional sriracha sauce.

**TO MAKE AHEAD** Sandwiches can be wrapped in plastic wrap and refrigerated up to 24 hours.

**PER SERVING** (1 wrap each) **CAL** 248, **FAT** 10 g (1 g sat. fat), **CHOL** 45 mg, **SODIUM** 601 mg, **CARB** 27 g (15 g fiber, 5 g sugars), **PRO** 23 g

Open-Face
Chicken
Sandwiches
with
Avocado
Slaw

## Poached Chicken Salad Sliders

**35g CARB** | **SERVES** 2
| **TOTAL** 25 min.

- 8 oz. chicken breast tenders
- ½ cup finely chopped celery
- ½ cup plain fat-free Greek yogurt
- 3 Tbsp. dried cranberries
- 1 Tbsp. chopped roasted, salted pistachio nuts
- ½ tsp. chopped fresh thyme
- ¼ tsp. kosher salt
- 2 cups mixed spring salad greens
- 2 tsp. olive oil
- 2 tsp. red wine vinegar or cider vinegar
- 4 1-oz. whole wheat cocktail buns
  Cracked black pepper (optional)

**1.** In a medium saucepan combine chicken and enough water to cover. Bring to boiling; reduce heat. Simmer, covered, 5 minutes or until chicken is done (165°F); drain. Shred chicken using two forks.

**2.** For chicken salad, in a bowl combine chicken and the next six ingredients (through salt). In another bowl combine greens, oil, and vinegar; toss to coat. Fill buns with spring greens and chicken salad. If desired, sprinkle with pepper.

**TIP** If desired, omit the buns and serve chicken salad over spring greens mixture.

**PER SERVING** *(2 sliders each)* **CAL** 414, **FAT** 12 g *(2 g sat. fat)*, **CHOL** 85 mg, **SODIUM** 472 mg, **CARB** 35 g *(5 g fiber, 16 g sugars)*, **PRO** 41 g

Thai Pork Wraps

## Thai Pork Wraps

**44g**
**CARB**

SERVES 6
TOTAL 30 min.

6  8- to 10-inch vegetable-flavor flour tortillas or plain flour tortillas
½  tsp. garlic salt
¼  to ½ tsp. black pepper
12  oz. pork tenderloin, cut into 1-inch strips
1  Tbsp. vegetable oil
4  cups shredded broccoli (broccoli slaw mix)
1  medium red onion, cut into thin wedges
1  tsp. grated fresh ginger
1  recipe Peanut Sauce

**1.** Preheat oven to 350°F. Wrap tortillas in foil. Bake about 10 minutes or until warm. Meanwhile, in a medium bowl combine garlic salt and pepper. Add pork; toss to coat.
**2.** In a large skillet cook and stir pork in hot oil over medium-high 4 to 6 minutes or until no longer pink. (Reduce heat if necessary to prevent overbrowning.) Remove pork from skillet; keep warm. Add broccoli, onion, and ginger to skillet. Cook and stir 4 to 6 minutes or until vegetables are crisp-tender. Remove from heat.
**3.** Spread Peanut Sauce over tortillas. Top with pork strips and vegetable mixture. Roll up tortillas. Serve immediately.

**TIP** Substitute 12 oz. skinless, boneless chicken breast strips for the pork.

**PEANUT SAUCE** In a small saucepan combine ¼ cup creamy peanut butter, 3 Tbsp. water, 1 Tbsp. sugar, 2 tsp. soy sauce, and 1 clove garlic, minced. Heat over medium-low, whisking constantly, until smooth and warm. Use immediately or keep warm over very low heat, stirring occasionally.

**PER SERVING** (1 wrap each) **CAL** 383, **FAT** 13 g (3 g sat. fat), **CHOL** 37 mg, **SODIUM** 661 mg, **CARB** 44 g (5 g fiber, 6 g sugars), **PRO** 22 g

Banh Mi
Sandwiches

## Banh Mi Sandwiches

**29g**
**CARB**

SERVES 6
TOTAL 30 min.

- 12 oz. natural pork tenderloin, trimmed and cut into ½-inch slices
- 1 to 2 Tbsp. sriracha or Asian sweet chili sauce
- 1 Tbsp. reduced-sodium soy sauce
  Nonstick cooking spray
- 1 small cucumber, seeded and cut into thin strips
- 1 small red bell pepper, cut into thin strips
- ½ cup shredded carrot
- ¼ cup chopped green onions
- 1 10-oz. loaf baguette-style French bread, split horizontally
- 1 recipe Sriracha Mayonnaise
- ¼ cup fresh cilantro leaves
- 1 fresh jalapeño pepper, thinly sliced and, if desired, seeded (tip, p. 154)

**1.** Lightly press pork slices to an even thickness. In a small bowl combine sriracha sauce and soy sauce; brush over pork. Coat a grill pan or extra-large skillet with cooking spray; heat pan over medium-high. Add pork; cook 4 to 6 minutes or until slightly pink in centers, turning once.
**2.** In a large bowl combine cucumber, sweet pepper, carrot, and green onions.
**3.** Spread bread with Sriracha Mayonnaise. Layer pork, vegetable mixture, cilantro, and jalapeño slices between bread halves. Cut into six portions.

**SRIRACHA MAYONNAISE** In a small bowl stir together ¼ cup light mayonnaise and 2 to 3 tsp. sriracha or Asian sweet chili sauce.

**PER SERVING** (1 portion each) **CAL** 230, **FAT** 5 g (1 g sat. fat), **CHOL** 40 mg, **SODIUM** 445 mg, **CARB** 29 g (3 g fiber, 3 g sugars), **PRO** 17 g

Turkey Apple Brie Sandwiches

## Turkey Apple Brie Sandwiches

**36g**
**CARB**

SERVES 4
TOTAL 20 min.

- 1⅓ cups thinly sliced Granny Smith apple
- 1 tsp. lemon juice
- 1 8-oz. loaf whole wheat baguette-style French bread
- 4 leaves red leaf lettuce
- 1 cup shredded cooked turkey breast tenderloin
- 2 oz. thinly sliced Brie cheese
- 4 tsp. Dijon mustard

**1.** In a small bowl toss together apple slices and lemon juice. Cut bread loaf into four portions; cut each portion in half horizontally. Remove soft insides of bread halves, leaving ¼-inch shells.

**2.** Layer bottom halves of bread with lettuce, turkey, apple slices, and cheese. Spread top halves of bread with mustard; place on top of sandwiches. Wrap and chill up to 4 hours.

**TIP** To cook turkey, in a skillet combine 1 turkey breast tenderloin and 1 cup water. Bring to boiling; reduce heat. Cover and simmer 20 to 25 minutes or until done (165°F). Shred using two forks. Store any remaining turkey in refrigerator up to 3 days or freeze up to 2 months.

**PER SERVING** (1 sandwich each) **CAL** 268, **FAT** 5 g (3 g sat. fat), **CHOL** 39 mg, **SODIUM** 413 mg, **CARB** 36 g (4 g fiber, 5 g sugars), **PRO** 19 g

Asian
Turkey
Lettuce
Wraps

## Ground Beef Gyros

**21g**
CARB

SERVES 4
TOTAL 20 min.

- 8 oz. 90%-lean ground beef
- 2 tsp. Greek seasoning
- ½ cup chopped seeded cucumber
- ½ cup chopped roma tomato
- ¼ cup thinly sliced red onion
- 2 Tbsp. chopped fresh parsley
- 1 Tbsp. lemon juice
- 2 tsp. olive oil
- ¼ tsp. salt
- ¼ tsp. black pepper
- 2 6-inch whole wheat pita bread rounds, halved crosswise
- ¼ cup plain fat-free Greek yogurt

**1.** In a large nonstick skillet cook ground beef and Greek seasoning over medium-high until browned. In a small bowl combine the next eight ingredients (through pepper).
**2.** Fill pita halves with meat and cucumber mixture. Top with yogurt.

**PER SERVING** (1 sandwich each) **CAL** 223, **FAT** 9 g (3 g sat. fat), **CHOL** 37 mg, **SODIUM** 400 mg, **CARB** 21 g (3 g fiber, 3 g sugars), **PRO** 16 g

## Asian Turkey Lettuce Wraps

**31g**
CARB

SERVES 4
TOTAL 15 min.

- 1 Tbsp. olive oil
- 1 lb. uncooked 93%-lean ground turkey
- 1 Tbsp. grated fresh ginger
- 2 cloves garlic, minced
- 1 8.8-oz. pouch cooked whole grain brown rice
- 2 Tbsp. hoisin sauce
- 1½ Tbsp. reduced-sodium soy sauce
- 1½ tsp. lime juice
- 1 8-oz. can sliced water chestnuts, drained and chopped
- 8 leaves romaine or butterhead lettuce
- ½ cup finely shredded carrot
- ⅓ cup chopped green onions
  Sesame seeds and lime wedges

**1.** In a large skillet heat oil over medium-high. Add turkey, ginger, and garlic; cook about 5 minutes or until turkey is browned. Reduce heat to medium.
**2.** Meanwhile, heat rice in a microwave according to package directions. In a small bowl stir together hoisin sauce, soy sauce, and lime juice.
**3.** Stir hoisin mixture, water chestnuts, and rice into skillet. Cook about 1 minute or until heated through.
**4.** Spoon turkey mixture onto lettuce leaves. Top evenly with carrot and green onions. Wrap lettuce around filling to eat. Sprinkle with sesame seeds and serve with lime wedges.

**TIP** Substitute 2 cups cooked cauliflower rice for the brown rice.

**PER SERVING** (2 wraps each) **CAL** 368, **FAT** 15 g (3 g sat. fat), **CHOL** 84 mg, **SODIUM** 476 mg, **CARB** 31 g (3 g fiber, 4 g sugars), **PRO** 25 g

Ground
Beef Gyros

Hot Beef
Sandwiches

## Hot Beef Sandwiches

**34g** CARB

**SERVES** 4
**HANDS ON** 30 min.
**TOTAL** 2 hr.

- Nonstick cooking spray
- 1 lb. beef stew meat, trimmed and cut into 1-inch cubes
- 1 14.5-oz. can unsalted beef broth
- 3 cloves garlic, minced
- ½ tsp. salt
- ¼ tsp. black pepper
- 2 cups 1-inch cubes peeled russet potatoes
- 2 cups small cauliflower florets
- ½ cup chopped carrot
- ¼ cup light sour cream
- ⅛ tsp. black pepper
- ¼ cup cold water
- 2 Tbsp. all-purpose flour
- 4 slices whole grain country-style bread, toasted
- ¼ cup sliced green onions

1. Coat a medium saucepan with cooking spray. Brown the stew meat, half at a time, over medium-high. Return all beef to pan. Add broth, two cloves of the garlic, ¼ tsp. of the salt, and the ¼ tsp. pepper. Bring to boiling; reduce heat. Simmer, covered, about 1½ hours or until very tender.
2. Meanwhile, in a separate medium saucepan combine potatoes and the remaining one clove garlic. Add enough water to cover by 1 inch. Bring to boiling; reduce heat. Cover and simmer 5 minutes. Add cauliflower and carrots. Return to boiling; reduce heat. Cover and simmer about 10 minutes more or until vegetables are very tender. Drain well.
3. In a large bowl combine vegetable mixture, sour cream, the remaining ¼ tsp. salt, and the ⅛ tsp. pepper. Mash mixture until light and fluffy.
4. Using a slotted spoon, remove meat from pan. Shred beef using two forks. If desired, strain beef cooking liquid through a fine-mesh sieve. Measure 1 cup liquid; return to pan and discard remaining liquid. In a small bowl stir together the cold water and flour until smooth. Stir into cooking liquid in pan. Cook and stir over medium until thickened and bubbly; cook and stir 1 minute more. Return shredded meat to pan; stir to combine.
5. Serve vegetable mash over toasted bread. Top with beef mixture. Sprinkle with green onions.

Better-Than-Takeout Burgers

**PER SERVING** (1 sandwich each) CAL 335, FAT 8 g (3 g sat. fat), CHOL 77 mg, SODIUM 555 mg, CARB 34 g (5 g fiber, 4 g sugars), PRO 33 g

## Better-Than-Takeout Burgers

**45g** CARB

**SERVES** 4
**HANDS ON** 35 min.
**TOTAL** 55 min.

- 1 lb. sweet potatoes, cut lengthwise into ½-inch wedges or strips
- 2 tsp. olive oil
- ¼ tsp. salt
- ¼ tsp. black pepper
- 12 oz. 90%-lean ground beef
- 1 cup finely chopped fresh button mushrooms
- 4 reduced-calorie whole wheat hamburger buns, such as Sara Lee Delightful, split
- 2 Tbsp. light mayonnaise
- 2 tsp. sriracha sauce
- 2 Tbsp. ketchup
- 4 lettuce leaves
- 2 roma tomatoes, sliced
- ½ cup sliced red onion

1. Preheat oven to 400°F. Line a 15×10-inch baking pan with parchment paper or a silicone baking mat. In the prepared pan toss sweet potatoes with oil and ⅛ tsp. each of the salt and pepper. Bake 40 to 45 minutes or until tender and browned, turning occasionally.
2. Meanwhile, in a medium bowl combine ground beef, mushrooms, and the remaining ⅛ tsp. each salt and pepper. Shape into 4½-inch patties. Grill, covered, over medium 10 to 12 minutes or until done (160°F), turning once. Grill buns, cut sides down, the last 1 minute or until toasted.
3. For mayonnaise sauce, in a small bowl stir together mayonnaise and 1 tsp. of the sriracha sauce. For ketchup sauce, in another small bowl stir together ketchup and the remaining 1 tsp. sriracha sauce.
4. Spread bottoms of buns with mayonnaise sauce. Fill buns with lettuce, tomatoes, burgers, and onion. Serve with sweet potatoes and ketchup sauce for dipping.

**PER SERVING** (1 burger + 10 sweet potato wedges each) CAL 408, FAT 15 g (4 g sat. fat), CHOL 58 mg, SODIUM 619 mg, CARB 45 g (11 g fiber, 12 g sugars), PRO 25 g

### Roast Beef 'n' Slaw Sandwiches

**21g**
**CARB**

**SERVES** 2
**TOTAL** 15 min.

- 2 Tbsp. light mayonnaise
- 1 Tbsp. cider vinegar
- 1 tsp. honey
- 1 tsp. horseradish mustard
- ⅛ tsp. caraway seeds, crushed
- ⅛ tsp. black pepper
- ¾ cup shredded cabbage with carrot (coleslaw mix)
- ¼ cup coarsely shredded carrot
- 3 oz. thinly sliced lower-sodium roast beef
- 4 very thin slices whole wheat bread, such as Pepperidge Farm
- 2 slices ultrathin sliced Swiss cheese, such as Sargento

**1.** In a medium bowl stir together the first six ingredients (through pepper). Add coleslaw mix and shredded carrot. Stir until well combined.

**2.** Arrange roast beef on two of the bread slices. Top with cheese, coleslaw mixture, and the remaining bread slices.

**PER SERVING** *(1 sandwich each)* **CAL** 244, **FAT** 10 g *(4 g sat. fat)*, **CHOL** 42 mg, **SODIUM** 511 mg, **CARB** 21 g *(3 g fiber, 7 g sugars)*, **PRO** 17 g

### TIP

Look for deli roast beef with less than 250 mg sodium per 2-oz. serving.

Salmon Burgers with Quick Pickled Cucumbers

## Salmon Burgers with Quick Pickled Cucumbers

**39g** CARB | **SERVES** 4
**TOTAL** 40 min.

- ½ cup water
- ½ cup white vinegar
- 2 Tbsp. honey
- ½ tsp. salt
- 1 English cucumber, thinly sliced (about 3 cups)
- 1 shallot, thinly sliced + 1 shallot, finely chopped
- 3 6-oz. cans no-salt-added salmon, drained and flaked
- 2 large eggs, lightly beaten
- ¼ cup panko
- 2 Tbsp. chopped fresh parsley
- 1 Tbsp. chopped fresh dill
- 1½ tsp. chopped fresh garlic
- 1 tsp. lemon zest
- ¼ tsp. black pepper
- 1 Tbsp. olive oil
- ¼ cup mayonnaise
- 4 whole wheat burger buns, split, and if desired, toasted

**1.** In a small saucepan combine water, vinegar, honey, and salt, Bring to boiling; remove from heat. In a medium bowl combine cucumber and sliced shallot. Pour vinegar mixture over vegetables.

**2.** In a large bowl stir together chopped shallot and the next eight ingredients (through pepper) until combined. Shape salmon mixture into four patties.
**3.** In a large nonstick skillet heat oil over medium. Add the patties and cook 8 to 10 minutes or until golden brown and done (145°F), turning once.
**4.** Drain the pickled vegetables. Spread mayonnaise on buns. Fill each with a salmon patty and about ¼ cup pickled vegetables. If desired, garnish with additional dill and serve with additional pickles.

**PER SERVING** (1 burger each) **CAL** 527, **FAT** 26 g (5 g sat. fat), **CHOL** 169 mg, **SODIUM** 747 mg, **CARB** 39 g (4 g fiber, 14 g sugars), **PRO** 34 g

Hummus
and
Tomato
Pitas

## Thai Veggie Pita Pockets

**36g** **SERVES** 4
**CARB** **HANDS ON** 25 min.
**TOTAL** 1 hr. 40 min.

- 1  15-oz. can no-salt-added garbanzo beans (chickpeas), rinsed and drained
- 2  Tbsp. olive oil
- ⅛  tsp. salt
- ⅛  tsp. black pepper
- 1  small sweet potato (7 oz.)
- 2  Tbsp. peanut sauce
- 1  Tbsp. lime juice
- 2  cloves garlic, peeled and halved
- 4  flax, oat bran, and whole wheat pita bread rounds, such as Joseph's, or low-carb pita bread rounds, halved
- 1  cup fresh baby spinach
- ½  cup matchstick-cut carrots
- 2  radishes, shredded

**1.** Preheat oven to 450°F. Place half of the garbanzo beans in a shallow baking pan. Drizzle with 1 Tbsp. of the oil and sprinkle with the salt and pepper; toss to coat. Roast, uncovered, 15 to 20 minutes or until crisp. Set aside to cool.
**2.** Meanwhile, prick the sweet potato with a fork. Microwave 4 to 5 minutes or until tender. Let cool; peel. Transfer pulp to a food processor or blender. Add the remaining garbanzo beans and 1 Tbsp. olive oil, the peanut sauce, lime juice, and garlic. Cover and process or blend until smooth (if necessary, add 2 to 3 Tbsp. water to make hummus spreadable).
**3.** Spread hummus in pita pocket halves. Add spinach, carrots, roasted garbanzo beans, and radishes.

**PER SERVING** *(2 pockets each)* **CAL** 255, **FAT** 10 g *(1 g sat. fat)*, **CHOL** 0 mg, **SODIUM** 459 mg, **CARB** 36 g *(10 g fiber, 6 g sugars)*, **PRO** 12 g

## Hummus and Tomato Pitas

**42g** **SERVES** 2
**CARB** **TOTAL** 15 min.

- 1  15-oz. can no-salt-added garbanzo beans (chickpeas), rinsed and drained
- ¼  cup lemon juice
- 1  tsp. ground cumin
- ¼  tsp. black pepper
- ⅛  tsp. salt
- 2  5-inch flax, oat bran, and whole wheat pita bread rounds, such as Joseph's
- 4  slices tomato
- ½  cup chopped seeded cucumber
- ⅓  cup finely chopped red onion
- 2  Tbsp. crumbled reduced-fat feta cheese

**1.** In a small bowl coarsely mash beans, lemon juice, cumin, pepper, and salt with a fork. Spread over pita bread. Top with the remaining ingredients.

**PER SERVING** *(1 pita each)* **CAL** 251, **FAT** 6 g *(1 g sat. fat)*, **CHOL** 5 mg, **SODIUM** 584 mg, **CARB** 42 g *(13 g fiber, 6 g sugars)*, **PRO** 17 g

Thai
Veggie
Pita
Pockets

# 5 SIMPLE
# SIDES &
# SALADS

These hardworking, nutrient-packed meal accompaniments shine on the side as they steal the show with color and flavor. What better way to get more fruits and vegetables than in juicy-fresh, cool Cucumber and Peach Salad with Pepita Pesto and cheesy Mexican Street Corn.

89

98

100

### Spring Pasta with Escarole

**45g** **CARB**  |  **SERVES** 4
**TOTAL** 35 min.

1  lb. asparagus, trimmed and cut into 2-inch pieces
4  oz. dried fettuccine or tagliatelle pasta
2  Tbsp. olive oil
1½  Tbsp. unsalted butter
1  large shallot, finely chopped
4  cloves garlic, minced
1  15-oz. can cannellini beans, rinsed and drained
2  tsp. lemon zest + additional for garnish
1  small head escarole, torn (about 12 oz.)
¼  cup grated Parmesan cheese
½  tsp. salt
½  tsp. black pepper
¼  tsp. crushed red pepper
    Lemon wedges

**1.** Bring a large pot of water to boiling. Add asparagus; cook about 3 minutes or until bright green. With a slotted spoon, transfer the asparagus to a colander; rinse under cold water and drain.

**2.** Add pasta to the boiling water; cook 8 to 10 minutes or until al dente. Reserve 1 cup pasta water. Drain pasta.

**3.** Add oil and butter to pot; heat over medium-high. Add shallot and garlic; cook and stir 2 to 3 minutes or until tender. Add asparagus, pasta, beans, lemon zest, and ¾ cup of the reserved pasta water. Cook about 4 minutes or until until a glossy sauce forms and coats the pasta, tossing and adding more pasta water as needed.

**4.** Add escarole, Parmesan, salt, black pepper, and crushed red pepper; toss to combine. Garnish with additional lemon zest and serve with lemon wedges.

**PER SERVING** *(1 ½ cups each)* **CAL** 330, **FAT** 13 g *(4 g sat. fat),* **CHOL** 16 mg, **SODIUM** 627 mg, **CARB** 45 g *(11 g fiber, 3 g sugars),* **PRO** 13 g

## Collard Greens with Shiitake Mushrooms

**11g CARB**

**SERVES** 4
**TOTAL** 25 min.

- ¾ **cup low-sodium vegetable broth**
- ¾ **tsp. smoked paprika**
- ¼ **tsp. ground cumin**
- ¼ **tsp. salt**
- ¼ **tsp. crushed red pepper**
- 2 **Tbsp. olive oil**
- 1 **5-oz. pkg. sliced shiitake mushrooms, coarsely chopped**
- 4 **cloves garlic, minced**
- 1 **16-oz. pkg. chopped collard greens**
- 2 **Tbsp. cider vinegar**
- 1 **tsp. hot sauce**
- ½ **tsp. black pepper**

**1.** In a small saucepan combine broth, paprika, cumin, salt, and crushed red pepper. Bring to a simmer; cook 1 minute. Remove from heat and keep warm.

**2.** In a large pot heat oil over medium-high. Add mushrooms and garlic; cook 4 to 6 minutes or until browned and tender, stirring frequently. Add 2 Tbsp. of the broth mixture to the pan and cook 1 minute more, scraping the bottom of the pan to loosen any browned bits.

**3.** Stir in collard greens, a few handfuls at a time. Cook and stir about 10 minutes, adding the broth mixture a few tablespoons at a time, until the greens are tender and the broth mixture is incorporated. (Reduce heat to medium if the mixture starts to boil too vigorously.)

**4.** Add vinegar, hot sauce, and black pepper; cook and stir 1 minute.

**PER SERVING** *(1 cup each)* **CAL** 120, **FAT** 8 g *(1 g sat. fat)*, **CHOL** 0 mg, **SODIUM** 227 mg, **CARB** 11 g *(6 g fiber, 2 g sugars)*, **PRO** 5 g

## Mexican Street Corn

**17g**
**CARB**

**SERVES** 8
**HANDS ON** 20 min.
**TOTAL** 1 hr. 50 min.

- 8 small ears sweet corn with husks
- 2 Tbsp. avocado oil or canola oil
- 1 tsp. chili powder
- ¼ tsp. cayenne pepper (optional)
- ⅛ tsp. salt
- ¾ cup crumbled Cotija cheese (3 oz.)
- ¼ cup chopped fresh cilantro
  Lime zest (optional)
  Lime wedges

**1.** Peel back corn husks, but do not remove. Remove silks; rinse corn. Fold husks back around corn. Tie husk tops with 100%-cotton kitchen string to secure. Soak corn in enough water to cover 1 to 2 hours; drain.

**2.** Grill corn, covered, over medium 30 to 35 minutes or until kernels are tender, turning once. Remove string and pull back husks. Tie husks with string to hold open.

**3.** Meanwhile, in a small bowl combine chili powder, cayenne pepper (if desired), and salt. Place corn on a platter and brush with oil. Sprinkle spice mixture over corn. Top with cheese, cilantro, and, if desired, lime zest. Serve with lime wedges.

**PER SERVING** (1 ear corn each) **CAL** 148, **FAT** 8 g (3 g sat. fat), **CHOL** 11 mg, **SODIUM** 208 mg, **CARB** 17 g (2 g fiber, 6 g sugars), **PRO** 5 g

Sesame
Sugar
Snaps

## Sesame Sugar Snaps

**9g**
**CARB**

SERVES 4
TOTAL 10 min.

- 2 8-oz. pkg. sugar snap pea pods (4 cups)
- 3 tsp. toasted sesame oil
- 1 cup shredded carrots
- 4 tsp. reduced-sodium soy sauce
- 2 cloves garlic, minced
- 1 tsp. grated fresh ginger
  Sesame seeds (optional)

**1.** Heat an extra-large heavy skillet over medium-high. Add pea pods and 1 tsp. of the oil; toss to coat. Cook 3 to 4 minutes or until peas start to blister, stirring occasionally. Add carrots; cook and stir 1 minute more.

**2.** In a small bowl whisk together soy sauce, garlic, ginger, and the remaining 2 tsp. oil; drizzle over vegetables. Cook and stir until heated through. If desired, sprinkle with sesame seeds.

**PER SERVING** *(1 cup each)* **CAL** 75, **FAT** 4 g *(1 g sat. fat)*, **CHOL** 0 mg, **SODIUM** 207 mg, **CARB** 9 g *(3 g fiber, 5 g sugars)*, **PRO** 2 g

Cabbage
and Apple
Farro Toss

## Cabbage and Apple Farro Toss

**23g**
**CARB**

SERVES 6
TOTAL 25 min.

- 3 cups shredded green cabbage
- 1 cup chopped apple
- ½ cup chopped onion
- 3 slices bacon, chopped
- 2 cups cooked farro, wild rice blend, or barley
- 2 Tbsp. cider vinegar
- 1 tsp. honey
- 1 tsp. Dijon mustard
- ¼ tsp. salt
- ¼ tsp. black pepper

**1.** In an extra-large skillet cook cabbage, apple, onion, and bacon over medium about 6 minutes or until onion is tender and bacon is crisp, stirring occasionally. Stir in the remaining ingredients.

**PER SERVING** (⅔ cup each) **CAL** 181, **FAT** 8 g (3 g sat. fat), **CHOL** 13 mg, **SODIUM** 256 mg, **CARB** 23 g (3 g fiber, 6 g sugars), **PRO** 5 g

## Grilled Prosciutto Peaches

**16g**
**CARB**

SERVES 4
TOTAL 10 min.

- 2 oz. soft goat cheese (chèvre)
- 2 large ripe peaches (1 lb.), halved and pitted
- 4 thin slices prosciutto
- 4 tsp. honey
  Chopped fresh mint

**1.** Spoon cheese onto cut sides of peach halves. Top with prosciutto, lightly pressing ends to adhere.
**2.** Grill, covered, over medium-high about 6 minutes or until prosciutto is browned and crisp, turning once. Drizzle with honey and sprinkle with mint.

**TIP** This recipe is easily multiplied to serve a crowd.

**PER SERVING** (1 peach half each) **CAL** 124, **FAT** 4 g (2 g sat. fat), **CHOL** 10 mg, **SODIUM** 244 mg, **CARB** 16 g (2 g fiber, 15 g sugars), **PRO** 6 g

Grilled Prosciutto Peaches

**TO MAKE AHEAD**

Prepare dressing as directed in Step 1. Cover and refrigerate up to 2 days.

## Green Goddess Broccoli Salad

**11g** CARB

**SERVES** 8
**TOTAL** 40 min.

- 1 **lemon**
- 3 **Tbsp. olive oil**
- 3 **cloves garlic, minced**
- ½ **cup low-fat mayonnaise**
- ¼ **cup low-fat buttermilk**
- ¼ **cup chopped fresh parsley**
- 1½ **Tbsp. chopped fresh chives**
- 1 **Tbsp. chopped fresh tarragon**
- 2 **oil-packed anchovy fillets, drained**

- ¼ **tsp. salt**
- ¼ **tsp. black pepper**
- 2 **heads broccoli (about 1¾ lb.), tops cut into small florets, stems peeled and cut into matchsticks**
- ½ **cup shredded carrot**
- 1 **Tbsp. unsalted dry-roasted sunflower kernels**

**1.** For dressing, remove 1 tsp. zest and squeeze 2 Tbsp. juice from lemon. In a small skillet heat oil and garlic over low 1 minute; transfer to a food processor. Add lemon zest and juice and the next eight ingredients (through pepper). Cover; process until smooth.

**2.** Bring a large pot of water to boiling. Add broccoli florets to the pot; cook 1 to 2 minutes or just until bright green and crisp-tender. Using a slotted spoon, immediately transfer florets to a large bowl of ice water. When cool, drain well and pat dry.

**3.** Combine broccoli florets, broccoli stems, and carrot in a large bowl. Add dressing; toss to coat. Sprinkle with sunflower kernels.

**PER SERVING** (about 1 cup each) **CAL** 112, **FAT** 7 g (1 g sat. fat), **CHOL** 1 mg, **SODIUM** 301 mg, **CARB** 11 g (5 g fiber, 2 g sugars), **PRO** 3 g

## White Beans and Tomatoes with Kale Pesto

**18g**
**CARB**

| **SERVES** 8 |
| **TOTAL** 20 min. |

- 1 **small lemon**
- 2 **tsp. olive oil**
- 1 **cup packed fresh baby kale**
- 2 **Tbsp. pine nuts, toasted**
- ¼ **cup finely shredded Parmesan cheese**
- 1 **clove garlic, peeled and halved**
- 1 **Tbsp. water**
- ½ **tsp. kosher salt**
- 3 **cups multicolor grape tomatoes, halved**
- 2 **15-oz. cans reduced-sodium cannellini beans, rinsed and drained**
- ½ **tsp. cracked black pepper**

**1.** For pesto, remove ½ tsp. zest and squeeze 1 Tbsp. juice from lemon. In a food processor combine zest, juice, 1 tsp. of the oil, and the next 6 ingredients (through salt). Cover and process until nearly smooth, stopping to scrape down sides as necessary.
**2.** Heat the remaining 1 tsp. oil in a large nonstick skillet over medium-high. Add tomatoes; cook about 2 minutes or until slightly soft, stirring occasionally. Add beans; cook about 3 minutes or until heated through, stirring occasionally. Stir in pepper. Serve bean mixture with pesto.

**PER SERVING** (½ cup bean mixture + 1 Tbsp. pesto each) **CAL** 122, **FAT** 3 g (1 g sat. fat), **CHOL** 2 mg, **SODIUM** 217 mg, **CARB** 17 g (5 g fiber, 2 g sugars), **PRO** 7 g

# veg out

You know eating more veggies is healthful,
but preparing them takes some planning.
Use this formula to cook up just about any vegetable
for a healthy side dish for four at around 100 calories
and no more than 15 grams of carbs per serving.

## THE BASE RECIPE

In a large skillet heat 2 Tbsp. olive oil over medium. Add 2 cloves garlic, minced; cook and stir about 30 seconds or until fragrant. Add 4 cups **VEGETABLE CHOICE** **1** and ¼ tsp. salt. Cook 7 to 10 minutes or until vegetables are tender and browned, stirring occasionally. Remove from heat. Toss vegetables with 1 Tbsp. **SOUR CHOICE** **2** and 1 Tbsp. chopped **FRESH HERB CHOICE** **3**. If desired, top servings with 2 Tbsp. freshly grated Parmesan cheese.

**1**
cauliflower
florets

**2**
rice wine
vinegar

**3**
fresh
cilantro

**SKILLET CARROTS**

1 ½-inch pieces carrot

2 red wine vinegar

3 fresh dill

**SKILLET SQUASH**

1 ¼-inch slices zucchini and yellow summer squash

2 fresh lemon juice

3 fresh basil

**SKILLET PEPPERS**

1 bite-size pieces red, orange, and/or yellow bell pepper

2 fresh lemon juice

3 fresh oregano

## Lemon-Dill Green Bean and Baby Potato Salad

**25g** CARB | **SERVES** 6 | **TOTAL** 40 min.

- 1 lemon
- 1½ Tbsp. white wine vinegar
- ½ tsp. Dijon mustard
- ¼ tsp. honey
- ¼ tsp. salt
- ½ tsp. black pepper
- 5 Tbsp. olive oil
- 2 Tbsp. chopped fresh dill
- 1½ lb. baby red potatoes
- 1 bay leaf
- 2 cloves garlic, peeled and smashed
- 12 oz. thin green beans (haricots verts) or regular green beans, trimmed and cut diagonally into 1½-inch pieces
- ½ cup finely chopped shallot

**1.** For dressing, remove 1 tsp. zest and squeeze 1½ Tbsp. juice from lemon. In a small bowl whisk together zest, juice, and the next five ingredients (through pepper). Whisking constantly, drizzle in 3 Tbsp. of the oil until combined. Whisk in dill.

**2.** Place potatoes, bay leaf, and garlic in a pot. Add cold water to cover by 1 inch. Bring to boiling; reduce heat. Simmer, uncovered, 7 to 10 minutes or until potatoes are tender. Using a slotted spoon, transfer the potatoes to a large bowl. Discard the bay leaf and garlic, but reserve the cooking water. When cool enough to handle, cut the potatoes into ½-inch pieces. Return to the bowl; toss with 3 Tbsp. of the dressing.

**3.** Return the pot of water to boiling; add green beans. Cook about 2 minutes or until crisp-tender. Using a slotted spoon, immediately transfer beans to a bowl of ice water to cool. Drain; pat dry.

**4.** In a small skillet cook shallot and oil over medium-low 30 seconds. Add to bowl with the potatoes. Add beans and the remaining dressing; toss to coat. If desired, garnish salad with additional fresh dill and lemon slices.

**TO MAKE AHEAD** Prepare dressing as directed in Step 1. Cover and refrigerate up to 2 days. Whisk well before tossing with salad.

**PER SERVING** *(1 cup each)* **CAL** 216, **FAT** 12 g *(2 g sat. fat)*, **CHOL** 0 mg, **SODIUM** 125 mg, **CARB** 25 g *(4 g fiber, 4 g sugars)*, **PRO** 4 g

## Grilled Eggplant and Summer Squash Salad

**7g** CARB | **SERVES** 8
**TOTAL** 50 min.

- ½ cup balsamic vinegar
- 1 medium eggplant (about 11 oz.)
- 1 medium yellow summer squash (about 8 oz.)
- 1 medium zucchini (about 10 oz.)
- ½ cup olive oil
- ¼ tsp. salt
- ½ tsp. black pepper
- 2 Tbsp. finely chopped pitted Kalamata olives
- 8 large fresh basil leaves

**1.** Place vinegar in a small saucepan. Bring to boiling; reduce heat. Simmer 12 to 15 minutes or until syrupy and reduced to about 2 Tbsp., stirring occasionally and watching carefully to prevent burning. Transfer to a small bowl and let cool.

**2.** Cut eggplant, yellow squash, and zucchini diagonally into ¼-inch slices. In a large bowl toss vegetables with 7 Tbsp. of the oil, the salt, and pepper.

**3.** Grill vegetables, uncovered, over medium-high 4 to 10 minutes or until tender and grill-marked, turning once.

**4.** Arrange vegetables on a platter. Drizzle with the remaining 1 Tbsp. oil and the reserved balsamic syrup. Top with olives and basil.

**TO MAKE AHEAD** Prepare balsamic drizzle as directed in Step 1. Cover and store at room temperature up to 1 day. Refrigerate vegetables up to 1 day.

**PER SERVING** (½ cup [about 4 slices] each)
**CAL** 161, **FAT** 14 g (2 g sat. fat), **CHOL** 0 mg, **SODIUM** 126 mg, **CARB** 7 g (2 g fiber, 5 g sugars), **PRO** 1 g

Tomato
and
Watermelon
Greek
Salad

## Tomato and Watermelon Greek Salad

**8g**
**CARB**

| SERVES | 6 |
|---|---|
| TOTAL | 15 min. |

- 2 Tbsp. olive oil
- 1½ Tbsp. red wine vinegar
- ¼ tsp. salt
- ¼ tsp. black pepper
- 3 cups torn romaine hearts
- 2 cups cherry tomatoes, halved
- 1 cup chopped orange bell pepper
- 1 cup cubed seedless watermelon
- 2 Tbsp. chopped fresh parsley
- 1 Tbsp. chopped fresh oregano
- 2 tsp. chopped fresh mint
- 15 pitted Kalamata olives, quartered lengthwise
- ½ cup crumbled feta cheese (2 oz.)

**1.** For dressing, in a large bowl whisk together oil, vinegar, salt, and black pepper.

**2.** Add the next seven ingredients (through mint) to the bowl; toss to coat. Add olives and feta; gently toss again. Serve immediately.

**PER SERVING** (1 cup each) **CAL** 131, **FAT** 10 g (3 g sat. fat), **CHOL** 11 mg, **SODIUM** 368 mg, **CARB** 8 g (2 g fiber, 5 g sugars), **PRO** 3 g

---

## Cucumber and Peach Salad with Pepita Pesto

**13g**
**CARB**

| SERVES | 6 |
|---|---|
| TOTAL | 20 min. |

- ⅓ cup unsalted roasted pumpkin seeds (pepitas)
- ½ cup fresh cilantro leaves
- ½ cup fresh parsley leaves
- 2 Tbsp. lime juice
- 1 Tbsp. coarsely chopped jalapeño pepper (tip, *p. 154*)
- 1 medium clove garlic, quartered
- ½ tsp. salt
- 2 Tbsp. olive oil
- 1½ English cucumbers, thinly sliced (about 4½ cups)
- 3 peaches, quartered and sliced
- ½ cup thinly sliced green onions
- 2 Tbsp. white wine vinegar

**1.** For pesto, place pepitas in a food processor: pulse until coarsely chopped. Add the next six ingredients (through salt); pulse until evenly chopped, scraping sides as needed. With the processor running, add oil in a steady stream until just combined but still chunky.

**2.** In a large bowl combine cucumbers, peaches, and green onions. Add pesto and vinegar; toss to coat. If desired, garnish with additional fresh parsley.

**PER SERVING** (1½ cups each) **CAL** 128, **FAT** 8 g (1 g sat. fat), **CHOL** 0 mg, **SODIUM** 201 mg, **CARB** 13 g (2 g fiber, 8 g sugars), **PRO** 4 g

Cucumber
and Peach
Salad with
Pepita Pesto

Potato-Cauliflower Salad with Horseradish Dressing

## Potato-Cauliflower Salad with Horseradish Dressing

**17g** CARB

SERVES 9
HANDS ON 20 min.
TOTAL 1 hr.

- 1½ lb. tiny new red and/or purple potatoes, halved or quartered
- 4 cups small cauliflower florets
- ½ cup plain fat-free Greek yogurt
- ¼ cup light mayonnaise
- 1 Tbsp. coarse-ground mustard
- 2 tsp. prepared horseradish
- 2 tsp. red wine vinegar
- ¼ tsp. salt
- ¼ tsp. black pepper
- 1 cup chopped red bell pepper
- ½ cup sliced green onions

**1.** In a 6-qt. Dutch oven cook potatoes in a large amount of boiling water 6 minutes. Add cauliflower; cook about 4 minutes more or just until vegetables are tender; drain. Rinse under cold water to cool; drain again.
**2.** In an extra-large bowl whisk together the next seven ingredients (through black pepper). Add cooked vegetables, bell pepper, and green onions; toss to coat. If desired, top with additional black pepper.

**PER SERVING** *(1 cup each)* **CAL** 100, **FAT** 2 g *(0 g sat. fat)*, **CHOL** 3 mg, **SODIUM** 166 mg, **CARB** 17 g *(3 g fiber, 3 g sugars)*, **PRO** 4 g

## Tomato Salad with Lemon-Basil Vinaigrette

**7g** CARB

SERVES 8
TOTAL 15 min.

- ¼ cup chopped fresh basil
- 3 Tbsp. lemon juice
- 2 Tbsp. olive oil
- 2 tsp. Dijon mustard
- ¼ tsp. salt
- ⅛ tsp. black pepper
- 4 large firm multicolor heirloom tomatoes, sliced
- 2 medium English cucumbers, thinly sliced
- ⅔ cup crumbled feta cheese (5 oz.)

**1.** In a large bowl whisk together the first six ingredients (through pepper). Add tomatoes and cucumbers; toss gently to coat. Arrange in a serving dish. Sprinkle with cheese and, if desired, additional basil.

**PER SERVING** *(1¼ cups each)* **CAL** 90, **FAT** 6 g *(2 g sat. fat)*, **CHOL** 11 mg, **SODIUM** 213 mg, **CARB** 7 g *(1 g fiber, 4 g sugars)*, **PRO** 3 g

Tomato
Salad with
Lemon-Basil
Vinaigrette

# 6
# EYE-OPENING
# BREAKFASTS

Protein and complex carbohydrates come together in wake-up foods that help sustain your energy all morning long. Make-ahead Fruit and Nut Freezer Oatmeal Cups to heat and eat help tame crazy mornings, and Spinach and Feta Egg Sandwiches are a take-out copycat made healthy.

105

109

118

Mediterranean
Egg and
Tomato Skillet
with Pita

## Mediterranean Egg and Tomato Skillet with Pita

**33g CARB**

**SERVES** 4
**HANDS ON** 30 min.
**TOTAL** 40 min.

- 2 Tbsp. olive oil
- 2 cups chopped red bell peppers
- ½ cup chopped onion
- 2 Tbsp. no-salt-added tomato paste
- 1 tsp. smoked paprika
- ½ tsp. crushed red pepper
- 3 cups chopped tomatoes
- 1 tsp. ground cumin
- ¼ tsp. salt
- 4 eggs
- ½ cup plain low-fat Greek yogurt
  Chopped fresh parsley
- 2 whole wheat pita bread rounds, halved crosswise and warmed

1. In a large skillet heat oil over medium. Add the next five ingredients (through crushed red pepper). Cook 5 to 7 minutes or until onion is tender, stirring occasionally. Stir in tomatoes, cumin, and salt. Bring to boiling; reduce heat. Simmer, uncovered, about 10 minutes or until tomatoes begin to break down.
2. Make four indentations in tomato mixture. Break eggs, one at a time, into a custard cup and slip into an indentation. Cover and simmer 4 to 6 minutes or until egg whites are completely set and yolks begin to thicken.
3. Top servings with yogurt and sprinkle with parsley. Serve with pita bread.

**PER SERVING** (1 cup tomato mixture and 1 egg each) **CAL** 303, **FAT** 13 g (3 g sat. fat), **CHOL** 189 mg, **SODIUM** 410 mg, **CARB** 33 g (6 g fiber, 11 g sugars), **PRO** 15 g

Apple, Bacon, and Sweet Potato Mini Casseroles

## Apple, Bacon, and Sweet Potato Mini Casseroles

**22g CARB**

**SERVES** 6
**HANDS ON** 30 min.
**TOTAL** 1 hr.

- Nonstick cooking spray
- 10 slices lower-sodium, less-fat bacon
- 2 cups chopped cooking apples
- ½ cup chopped onion
- 1 10-oz. sweet potato, peeled and cut into ¼-inch pieces
- 2 tsp. chopped fresh thyme or ½ tsp. dried thyme, crushed
- ¼ tsp. black pepper
- 1½ cups refrigerated or frozen egg product, thawed, or 6 eggs, lightly beaten
- ¾ cup fat-free milk
- ¾ cup shredded reduced-fat cheddar cheese (3 oz.)

1. Preheat oven to 350°F. Coat twelve 2½-inch muffin cups with cooking spray. Cut four of the bacon slices crosswise into thirds; chop the remaining bacon.
2. In an extra-large skillet cook large bacon pieces over medium until crisp. Drain bacon on paper towels; discard drippings. Add chopped bacon, apples, and onion to skillet. Cook over medium 5 minutes, stirring occasionally. Add sweet potato; cook about 10 minutes or just until potato is tender, stirring frequently. Stir in thyme and pepper.
3. Divide potato mixture among the prepared muffin cups. In a medium bowl whisk together egg and milk; pour over potato mixture (cups will be full). Top with cheese.
4. Bake about 25 minutes or until puffed and a knife inserted in centers comes out clean. Cool in cups 5 minutes. Remove from cups. Top with large bacon pieces. Serve warm.

**PER SERVING** (2 mini casseroles each) **CAL** 198, **FAT** 6 g (3 g sat. fat), **CHOL** 16 mg, **SODIUM** 387 mg, **CARB** 22 g (3 g fiber, 11 g sugars), **PRO** 15 g

Veggie,
Bacon, and
Quinoa Quiche
Wedges

**OUT THE DOOR**

To make this a handheld meal, wrap the wide end of a heated quiche wedge with parchment paper or foil.

## Veggie, Bacon, and Quinoa Quiche Wedges

**16g CARB**

**SERVES** 6
**HANDS ON** 25 min.
**TOTAL** 1 hr. 20 min.

Nonstick cooking spray
½ cup quinoa, rinsed and drained
1 Tbsp. olive oil
2 cups sliced fresh mushrooms
½ cup sliced leek
1 cup loosely packed coarsely chopped fresh spinach
4 slices applewood-smoked bacon, crisp-cooked and coarsely crumbled
4 eggs, lightly beaten
1½ cups fat-free milk
½ cup shredded Gruyère or Havarti cheese (2 oz.)
¼ tsp. salt
⅛ tsp. black pepper

1. Preheat oven to 350°F. Coat a 9-inch pie plate with cooking spray. Spread uncooked quinoa in bottom of prepared pie plate.
2. In a large skillet heat olive oil over medium. Add mushrooms and leek; cook and stir 3 to 5 minutes or until just tender. Remove from heat. Stir in spinach and bacon.
3. Spread mushroom mixture over quinoa. In a medium bowl whisk together eggs, milk, cheese, salt, and pepper. Pour over mixture in pie plate (dish will be full).

4. Bake 45 to 50 minutes or until center is set and top is golden.

**TO MAKE AHEAD** Cool quiche completely; cut into wedges. Wrap individual wedges with plastic wrap and store in the refrigerator up to 3 days. To freeze, overwrap with foil; freeze up to 1 month. To reheat, unwrap a chilled or frozen quiche wedge and place on a microwave-safe plate. Cover and microwave about 1½ minutes or until heated through.

**PER SERVING** (1 wedge each) **CAL** 205, **FAT** 10 g (3 g sat. fat), **CHOL** 136 mg, **SODIUM** 307 mg, **CARB** 16 g (2 g fiber, 5 g sugars), **PRO** 13 g

## Asparagus-Mushroom Toast Cups

**17g CARB**

SERVES 6
HANDS ON 20 min.
TOTAL 50 min.

Butter-flavor nonstick cooking spray

12 very thin slices whole wheat bread, such as Pepperidge Farm

2 tsp. canola oil

1 cup sliced fresh cremini or button mushrooms

6 oz. fresh asparagus, trimmed and cut into bite-size pieces

6 links cooked chicken-and-maple or turkey breakfast sausage, chopped

1¼ cups refrigerated or frozen egg product, thawed, or 5 eggs, lightly beaten

½ cup fat-free milk

1 tsp. Dijon mustard

½ tsp. chopped fresh thyme or ⅛ tsp. dried thyme, crushed

1. Preheat oven to 350°F. Coat twelve 2½-inch muffin cups with cooking spray. If desired, use a rolling pin to slightly flatten bread slices. Lightly coat both sides of bread with cooking spray. Line prepared muffin cups with bread.

2. In a large skillet heat oil over medium. Add mushrooms; cook 3 minutes, stirring occasionally. Add asparagus; cook 3 to 4 minutes more or just until vegetables are tender, stirring frequently. Stir in sausage.

3. Divide sausage mixture among muffin cups. In a medium bowl whisk together egg, milk, mustard, and thyme; pour over sausage mixture.

4. Bake 25 to 30 minutes or until puffed and a knife inserted in centers comes out clean. Cool in cups 5 minutes. Remove from cups. Serve warm.

PER SERVING *(2 toast cups each)* **CAL** 166, **FAT** 5 g *(1 g sat. fat),* **CHOL** 15 mg, **SODIUM** 398 mg, **CARB** 17 g *(3 g fiber, 5 g sugars),* **PRO** 12 g

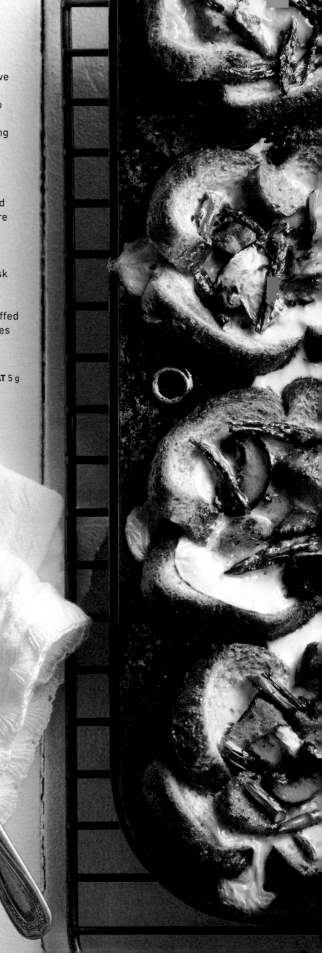

Spinach and
Feta Egg
Sandwiches

Broccoli-
Cheddar Egg
Sandwiches

## Spinach and Feta Egg Sandwiches

**28g CARB**

**SERVES** 12
**HANDS ON** 15 min.
**TOTAL** 35 min.

**Nonstick cooking spray**
- 1 **10-oz. pkg. frozen chopped spinach, thawed and squeezed dry**
- 1 **cup chopped red or orange bell pepper**
- 1 **cup crumbled feta cheese (4 oz.)**
- 10 **eggs**
- ⅓ **cup reduced-fat milk**
- 1 **tsp. dried dill**
- ¼ **tsp. salt**
- ¼ **tsp. black pepper**
- 12 **whole grain or whole wheat English muffins, split and toasted**

**1.** Preheat oven to 375°F. Coat a 15×10-inch baking pan with cooking spray. Spread spinach, bell pepper, and cheese in prepared pan. In a medium bowl whisk together eggs, milk, dill, salt, and black pepper. Pour egg mixture over vegetable mixture in pan.
**2.** Bake about 15 minutes or until edges are puffed and center is set. Cool in pan 5 minutes. Cut into 12 portions. Fill each English muffin with an egg portion.

**PER SERVING** *(1 sandwich each)* **CAL** 226, **FAT** 7 g *(3 g sat. fat)*, **CHOL** 164 mg, **SODIUM** 428 mg, **CARB** 28 g *(3 g fiber, 2 g sugars)*, **PRO** 11 g

## Broccoli-Cheddar Egg Sandwiches

**26g CARB**

**SERVES** 12
**HANDS ON** 15 min.
**TOTAL** 35 min.

**Nonstick cooking spray**
- 2½ **cups frozen broccoli florets, thawed and cut into bite-size pieces**
- ½ **cup chopped roasted red bell pepper**
- 10 **eggs**
- ⅓ **cup reduced-fat milk**
- ½ **tsp. kosher salt**
- ¼ **tsp. black pepper**
- 1½ **cups shredded cheddar cheese (6 oz.)**
- 12 **whole grain English muffins, split and toasted**
- 2 **roma tomatoes, sliced (optional)**
- ¼ **cup basil pesto (optional)**

**1.** Preheat oven to 375°F. Coat a 15×10-inch baking pan with cooking spray. Spread broccoli and roasted pepper in the prepared pan. In a medium bowl whisk together eggs, milk, salt, and black pepper. Pour egg mixture over vegetables in pan; sprinkle with cheese.
**2.** Bake about 15 minutes or until edges are puffed and center is set. Cool in pan 5 minutes. Cut into 12 portions.
**3.** Fill each English muffin with an egg portion and, if desired, 2 tomato slices and/or 1 tsp. of the pesto.

**PER SERVING** *(1 sandwich each)* **CAL** 252, **FAT** 10 g *(4 g sat. fat)*, **CHOL** 170 mg, **SODIUM** 488 mg, **CARB** 26 g *(4 g fiber, 3 g sugars)*, **PRO** 16 g

### TO MAKE AHEAD

Layer cooled egg portions between waxed paper in an airtight container. Store in refrigerator up to 3 days or freeze up to 1 month. To reheat, wrap one chilled or frozen egg portion at a time in waxed paper. Microwave chilled portion 30 seconds, frozen portion 1 minute, or until heated through, turning once.

## Individual Sausage and Cauliflower Crustless Quiches

**8g CARB**

SERVES 2
HANDS ON 20 min.
TOTAL 45 min.

Nonstick cooking spray
1 Tbsp. vegetable oil
1 cup fresh cauliflower rice
3 oz. cooked dried tomato-and-basil or spinach-and-feta chicken sausage, chopped
4 medium asparagus spears, trimmed and cut into ½-inch pieces
¼ cup chopped onion
2 Tbsp. finely shredded Parmesan cheese
1 egg
2 egg whites
2 Tbsp. reduced-fat milk
½ tsp. dried Italian seasoning, crushed
⅛ tsp. black pepper
Torn fresh basil (optional)

**1.** Preheat oven to 350°F. Coat four 6-oz. custard cups with cooking spray. In a large skillet heat oil over medium. Add cauliflower rice, sausage, asparagus, and onion; cook 4 to 6 minutes or until asparagus is crisp-tender, stirring frequently. Remove from heat. Stir in cheese. Divide mixture among prepared custard cups.
**2.** In a medium bowl whisk together the remaining ingredients. Slowly pour egg mixture over cauliflower mixture. If needed, gently press cauliflower mixture down lightly to moisten.
**3.** Bake about 20 minutes or until a knife inserted in centers comes out clean. Cool in custard cups on a wire rack 5 minutes. If desired, loosen sides; remove from cups and sprinkle with basil. Serve warm.

**TO MAKE AHEAD** Place cooled quiches in an airtight container and store in the refrigerator up to 3 days. To reheat, microwave one quiche at a time on 50% power 1 to 2 minutes or until warm.

**PER SERVING** *(2 quiches each)* **CAL** 243, **FAT** 14 g *(4 g sat. fat)*, **CHOL** 133 mg, **SODIUM** 564 mg, **CARB** 8 g *(2 g fiber, 5 g sugars)*, **PRO** 19 g

Individual
Sausage and
Cauliflower
Crustless
Quiches

## Mini Bacon and Egg Bakes

**1g CARB**

**SERVES** 12
**HANDS ON** 25 min.
**TOTAL** 55 min.

Nonstick cooking spray
12 slices bacon
9 eggs
⅓ cup reduced-fat milk
2 cloves garlic, minced
½ tsp. salt
¼ tsp. black pepper
2 to 3 cups chopped fresh spinach
¾ cup shredded white cheddar cheese (3 oz.)
1 roma tomato, cut into 12 slices

**1.** Preheat oven to 375°F. Coat twelve 2½-inch muffin cups with cooking spray. In a large skillet cook bacon over medium 5 to 7 minutes or until cooked through but still pliable and just starting to brown. Drain on paper towels; cool slightly.

**2.** Wrap one slice of bacon around the inside of each muffin cup. In a large bowl whisk together eggs, milk, garlic, salt, and pepper. Stir in spinach and cheese. Divide mixture among muffin cups.

**3.** Top each egg mixture with a tomato slice. Bake 20 to 25 minutes or until egg mixture is puffed and set. Cool in muffin cups 5 minutes (mixture may fall slightly during cooling). Loosen sides; remove from cups. Serve warm.

**TO MAKE AHEAD** Place cooled egg bakes in an airtight container and store in the refrigerator up to 3 days. To reheat, microwave one egg bake at a time on 50% power 1 to 2 minutes or until internal temperature reaches 165°F.

**PER SERVING** (1 egg bake each) **CAL** 126, **FAT** 9 g (4 g sat. fat), **CHOL** 155 mg, **SODIUM** 335 mg, **CARB** 1 g (0 g fiber, 1 g sugars), **PRO** 10 g

Pumpkin
Breakfast
Bread
Puddings

Squash Breakfast Bowls

## Pumpkin Breakfast Bread Puddings

**21g**
**CARB**

**SERVES** 6
**HANDS ON** 20 min.
**TOTAL** 45 min.

Nonstick cooking spray
- 2 egg whites
- 1 egg
- ½ cup canned pumpkin
- ½ cup fat-free milk
- 2 Tbsp. pure maple syrup
- ½ tsp. ground cinnamon
- ⅛ tsp. salt
- ⅛ tsp. ground nutmeg
  Dash ground cloves
- 6 slices high-fiber whole wheat bread, cut into 1-inch pieces (6 cups)
- ¼ cup chopped toasted pecans
- 2 tsp. butter
- 2 Tbsp. pure maple syrup

**1.** Preheat oven to 375°F. Lightly coat six 6-oz. ramekins or custard cups with cooking spray. In a large bowl whisk together the next nine ingredients (through cloves). Stir in bread pieces and pecans. Divide mixture among the prepared ramekins. Arrange ramekins in a shallow baking pan.

**2.** Bake about 25 minutes or until lightly browned on top and 160°F in centers. Cool slightly. Serve warm topped with butter and the syrup.

**PER SERVING** *(1 pudding each)* **CAL** 149, **FAT** 6 g *(1 g sat. fat)*, **CHOL** 39 mg, **SODIUM** 182 mg, **CARB** 21 g *(3 g fiber, 11 g sugars)*, **PRO** 6 g

## Squash Breakfast Bowls

**29g**
**CARB**

**SERVES** 4
**HANDS ON** 15 min.
**TOTAL** 50 min.

- 1 2-lb. butternut squash, halved lengthwise and seeded
- 2 tsp. olive oil
- 4 slices bacon, crisp-cooked and crumbled
- ½ tsp. chili powder
- ½ tsp. ground coriander
- ¼ tsp. sea salt
- ¼ tsp. black pepper
- 2 cups mixed berries, such as blackberries, blueberries, raspberries, and/or halved strawberries
- ¼ cup roasted salted pumpkin seeds (pepitas)
- 2 Tbsp. pure maple syrup

**1.** Preheat oven to 400°F. Line a baking sheet with foil. Brush cut sides of squash with oil. Place squash halves, cut sides down, on prepared baking sheet. Roast 35 to 40 minutes or until very tender; cool slightly. Scrape squash flesh from skins; discard skins.

**2.** Measure 2 cups squash and add to a medium bowl. (Store any extra squash in an airtight container in the refrigerator up to 3 days.) Stir in bacon, chili powder, coriander, salt, and pepper.

**3.** Divide squash mixture among bowls. Top with berries and pepitas and drizzle with maple syrup.

**TIP** Save some time and use frozen cubed butternut squash. Skip Step 1 and cook according to package instructions.

**TIP** To roast your own pumpkin seeds, preheat oven to 350°F. Rinse the seeds under running water to clean off attached pulp. Shake off excess water; spread seeds on a lightly greased baking sheet. Lightly sprinkle with sea salt or other dried seasonings, then bake 15 minutes or until brown. Roasted squash seeds also make an excellent high-protein snack.

**PER SERVING** *(½ cup squash + ½ cup berries + 1 Tbsp. pepitas each)* **CAL** 242, **FAT** 12 g *(3 g sat. fat)*, **CHOL** 8 mg, **SODIUM** 325 mg, **CARB** 29 g *(7 g fiber, 14 g sugars)*, **PRO** 9 g

## Quick Skillet Granola

**16g CARB**

**SERVES** 8
**TOTAL** 15 min.

- ⅔ cup regular rolled oats
- ¼ cup slivered almonds
- 2 Tbsp. flaxseeds
- 1 Tbsp. canola oil
- 1 Tbsp. honey
- ½ tsp. ground cinnamon
  Pinch salt
- ⅓ cup banana chips, coarsely crushed
- ⅓ cup 50%-less-sugar dried cranberries (such as Ocean Spray)
  Reduced-fat milk, yogurt, and/or fresh fruit (optional)

1. Heat a large nonstick skillet over medium. Add oats and almonds. Cook 3 to 5 minutes or until mixture is lightly browned, stirring frequently. (Reduce heat to medium-low if mixture browns too quickly.) Stir in flaxseeds, oil, honey, cinnamon, and salt. Cook and stir 1 minute more or until most of the liquid is absorbed and the almonds and oats are golden brown.
2. Remove from heat. Spread on waxed paper to cool. If desired, serve in bowls with milk or yogurt and fresh fruit.

**TO STORE** Place cooled granola in an airtight container. Store at room temperature up to 1 week.

**PER SERVING** *(¼ cup each)* **CAL** 114, **FAT** 6 g *(1 g sat. fat)*, **CHOL** 0 mg, **SODIUM** 19 mg, **CARB** 16 g *(4 g fiber, 6 g sugars)*, **PRO** 2 g

Quick Skillet Granola

**TIP**

Boost the flavor by adding a dash of cinnamon or a few drops of lemon or orange extract.

## Overnight Blueberry Oats

**35g**
**CARB**

SERVES 2
HANDS ON 10 min.
TOTAL 2 hr. 10 min.

- ⅔ cup fresh blueberries
- ⅔ cup regular rolled oats
- ⅔ cup refrigerated original unsweetened almond milk
- ⅓ cup plain low-fat Greek yogurt
- 1 Tbsp. pure maple syrup
- 1 tsp. lemon zest
- ⅛ tsp. salt
- ⅛ tsp. almond or vanilla extract
- 1 Tbsp. slivered almonds, toasted

**1.** In a jar or bowl lightly mash blueberries with a fork or the handle of a spoon. Add the next seven ingredients (through almond extract); stir to combine. Cover and chill at least 2 hours or overnight. Top servings with almonds and, if desired, additional fresh blueberries.

**TO STORE** Transfer to an airtight container. Store in refrigerator up to 3 days.

PER SERVING (¾ cup each) CAL 216, FAT 6 g (1 g sat. fat), CHOL 3 mg, SODIUM 220 mg, CARB 35 g (5 g fiber, 13 g sugars), PRO 9 g

## Crunchy Honey-Nut Breakfast Cereal

**37g CARB**

| | |
|---|---|
| **SERVES** | 12 |
| **HANDS ON** | 10 min. |
| **TOTAL** | 1 hr. 35 min. |

- 2 cups bite-size rice square cereal
- 2 cups regular rolled oats
- 2 cups sliced or slivered almonds
- 1 cup bran flakes cereal
- 1 cup round toasted oat cereal
- 1 cup coarsely chopped pecans
- ¼ cup canola oil
- ¼ cup honey
- 1½ tsp. ground cinnamon
- ¼ tsp. salt
- ¼ cup chia seeds or hemp seeds
- 6 cups reduced-fat milk

**1.** Preheat oven to 350°F. In a large roasting pan toss together the first six ingredients (through pecans). In a small bowl whisk together next four ingredients (through salt) until well combined. Pour over cereal mixture in pan. Toss to coat.
**2.** Bake 15 minutes, stirring once halfway through. Stir in seeds. Bake 5 to 10 minutes more or until cereal mixture is lightly browned. Spread cereal mixture onto a large sheet of parchment paper; cool completely.
**3.** Store cereal mixture in an airtight container in a cool, dry place up to 2 weeks. Or to freeze, divide cereal mixture among two or three freezer bags; freeze up to 2 months.
**4.** Serve cereal in bowls with milk.

**PER SERVING** (¾ cup cereal + ½ cup milk each)
**CAL** 394, **FAT** 24 g (3 g sat. fat), **CHOL** 10 mg,
**SODIUM** 170 mg, **CARB** 37 g (7 g fiber,
14 g sugars), **PRO** 12 g

Crunchy
Honey-Nut
Breakfast
Cereal

Fruit and Nut Freezer Oatmeal Cups

## Honey-Glazed Pumpkin-Banana Bread

**31g CARB**

**SERVES** 32
**HANDS ON** 25 min.
**TOTAL** 1 hr. 25 min.

- 3⅓ cups all-purpose flour
- 2 tsp. baking soda
- 1½ tsp. salt
- 1 tsp. baking powder
- 1 tsp. ground cinnamon
- 1 tsp. ground ginger
- 2 cups sugar
- ⅔ cup vegetable oil
- 4 eggs
- ⅔ cup water
- 1 15-oz. can pumpkin
- ½ cup mashed ripe banana
- 1 recipe Honey Glaze
- 2 Tbsp. finely chopped crystallized ginger

**1.** Preheat oven to 350°F. Grease bottoms and ½ inch up sides of two 9×5-inch loaf pans. In a medium bowl stir together first six ingredients (through ginger).
**2.** In an extra-large bowl beat sugar and oil with a mixer on medium until combined. Add eggs, one at a time, beating after each addition. Alternately add flour mixture and the water, beating on low after each addition just until combined. Beat in pumpkin and banana. Spread batter in prepared pans.
**3.** Bake 50 to 60 minutes or until a toothpick comes out clean. Cool in pans on wire racks 10 minutes. Remove from pans; cool completely on wire racks. Wrap and store overnight.
**4.** To serve, spoon Honey Glaze over loaves and sprinkle with crystallized ginger.

**HONEY GLAZE** In a small bowl beat ¼ cup honey and 2 Tbsp. softened butter with a mixer on medium until combined. Beat in 1 cup powdered sugar. Beat in enough milk (about 1 tsp.) to reach thick drizzling consistency.

**PER SERVING** (1 slice each) **CAL** 184, **FAT** 6 g (1 g sat. fat), **CHOL** 25 mg, **SODIUM** 219 mg, **CARB** 31 g (1 g fiber, 19 g sugars), **PRO** 2 g,

## Fruit and Nut Freezer Oatmeal Cups

**22g CARB**

**SERVES** 12
**HANDS ON** 15 min.
**TOTAL** 6 hr. 25 min.

- 5 cups water
- ½ tsp. salt
- 2 cups regular rolled oats
- ⅓ cup packed brown sugar
- 1 Tbsp. butter
- 1 tsp. ground cinnamon
- ½ cup dried fruit, such as unsweetened cherries, cranberries, raisins, and/or snipped apricots
- 1 cup fresh berries, such as blueberries, raspberries, and/or chopped strawberries
- ½ cup chopped toasted nuts, such as almonds, walnuts, and/or pecans
  Reduced-fat milk (optional)

**1.** In a medium saucepan bring the water and salt to boiling; stir in oats. Reduce heat to medium; cook 5 minutes, stirring occasionally. (Mixture will be thin but will thicken as it cools.) Remove from heat. Stir in brown sugar, butter, and cinnamon. Transfer to a bowl. Cover and chill until cool. Stir in dried fruit.
**2.** Grease twelve 2½-inch muffin cups. Mound about ½ cup of the oatmeal into each prepared cup. Sprinkle with berries and nuts; press lightly. Cover and freeze 6 hours or until firm. Let stand at room temperature 5 minutes. Transfer oatmeal cups to freezer bags or airtight containers. Freeze up to 3 months.
**3.** To serve, in a small bowl microwave one frozen oatmeal cup at a time, covered, 2 minutes or until heated through, stirring once. Stir before serving. If desired, serve with milk.

**PER SERVING** (1 oatmeal cup each) **CAL** 132, **FAT** 4 g (1 g sat. fat), **CHOL** 3 mg, **SODIUM** 110 mg, **CARB** 22 g (3 g fiber, 11 g sugars), **PRO** 3 g

Honey-Glazed
Pumpkin-Banana
Bread

**TO FREEZE**

Place cooled
loaves in freezer
bags and freeze up to
3 months. To serve,
thaw wrapped loaves
in refrigerator
overnight.

# 7

# GOOD-FOR-YOU SNACKS

Don't forget the snacks! These easy treats curb between-meal munchies with nutrient-rich options like Chili-Lime Zucchini Chips and high-fiber Green Pea-Chimichurri Dip. For away-from-home snacking, pack satisfying no-bake Carrot Cake Energy Bites.

125

126

132

Chili-Lime
Zucchini
Chips

## Chili-Lime Zucchini Chips

**8g**
**CARB**

**SERVES** 2
**HANDS ON** 20 min.
**TOTAL** 2 hr. 15 min.

- 2 **medium zucchini, trimmed (about 7 oz. each)**
  **Nonstick cooking spray**
- 2 **tsp. lime juice**
- ¼ **tsp. chili powder**
- ¼ **tsp. salt**

**1.** Position racks in the upper and lower thirds of oven. Preheat oven to 225°F. Line two large baking sheets with parchment paper.
**2.** Slice zucchini ⅛ inch thick (a mandoline slicer is useful for this). Arrange the slices in a single layer on the prepared pans and pat dry with paper towels. (The slices can be close to each other but should not overlap.) Lightly coat zucchini with cooking spray. Sprinkle with lime juice, chili powder, and salt.

**3.** Bake 1 hour, switching the positions of the pans halfway through. Turn the zucchini slices over and continue baking 45 to 55 minutes more or until golden and no longer damp. (After the first hour, check every 5 to 10 minutes and remove any darker slices as they are done.) Transfer the zucchini chips to a wire rack to cool.

**TO MAKE AHEAD** Place chips in an airtight container and store at room temperature up to 1 day. If chips lose their crunch, spread them on a baking sheet and toast briefly in the oven or in an air fryer to crisp.

**PER SERVING** *(1 scant cup each)* **CAL** 72, **FAT** 4 g *(0 g sat. fat)*, **CHOL** 0 mg, **SODIUM** 319 mg, **CARB** 8 g *(2 g fiber, 5 g sugars)*, **PRO** 2 g

## Lemony Butter Bean Lettuce Cups

**14g**
**CARB**

**SERVES** 4
**TOTAL** 10 min.

- 1 **lemon**
- 1 **Tbsp. olive oil**
- 1 **Tbsp. chopped fresh mint**
- ¼ **tsp. salt**
- ¼ **tsp. black pepper**
- 1 **15-oz. can no-salt-added butter beans, rinsed and drained**
- 1 **Tbsp. finely chopped shallot**
- 4 **butterhead (Boston or Bibb) lettuce leaves**

**1.** Remove 1 tsp. zest and squeeze 2 Tbsp. juice from lemon. In a bowl whisk together zest, juice, olive oil, mint, salt, and pepper. Add beans and shallot; stir to coat. Spoon bean mixture into lettuce leaves.

**PER SERVING** *(1 cup each)* **CAL** 110, **FAT** 4 g *(0 g sat. fat)*, **CHOL** 0 mg, **SODIUM** 173 mg, **CARB** 14 g *(3 g fiber, 0 g sugars)*, **PRO** 4 g

Lemony
Butter Bean
Lettuce Cups

## Green Pea-Chimichurri Dip

**19g**
**CARB**

**SERVES** 8
**HANDS ON** 15 min.
**TOTAL** 20 min.

1½ cups shelled fresh English peas
½ of a 12-oz. pkg. soft silken-style tofu
1 cup packed fresh parsley leaves
2 Tbsp. olive oil
2 Tbsp. red wine vinegar
2 cloves garlic
½ tsp. salt
¼ tsp. crushed red pepper
¼ tsp. black pepper
Toasted baguette-style French bread slices and/or assorted vegetable dippers

**1.** In a medium saucepan cook peas in boiling water about 5 minutes or just until tender and bright green; drain. Immediately plunge peas in a bowl of ice water to cool; drain well.
**2.** In a food processor combine peas and the next eight ingredients (through black pepper). Cover and process until nearly smooth. Serve dip with baguette slices and/or vegetables.

**PER SERVING** (¼ cup dip each) **CAL** 133, **FAT** 4 g (1 g sat. fat), **CHOL** 0 mg, **SODIUM** 260 mg, **CARB** 19 g (4 g fiber, 5 g sugars), **PRO** 5 g

### Watermelon Fruit Pizza

**25g**
**CARB**

**SERVES** 4
**HANDS ON** 15 min.
**TOTAL** 15 min.

- **1** 1-inch-thick slice watermelon, cut from the center of a large watermelon
- **½** cup plain low-fat Greek yogurt
- **2** tsp. honey
- **½** tsp. lime zest
- **¼** cup unsweetened shredded coconut, lightly toasted
- **¼** cup coarsely chopped salted shelled, roasted pistachio nuts
- **¼** cup chopped fresh mint

**1.** Cut watermelon slice into eight equal wedges; remove seeds. Place wedges 1 inch apart on a platter. In a small bowl whisk together yogurt, honey, and lime zest. Spoon over watermelon wedges. Sprinkle evenly with coconut, pistachio nuts, and mint. Serve immediately.

**PER SERVING** *(2 wedges each)* **CAL** 173, **FAT** 7 g *(3 g sat. fat)*, **CHOL** 3 mg, **SODIUM** 49 mg, **CARB** 25 g *(3 g fiber, 19 g sugars)*, **PRO** 6 g

Watermelon Fruit Pizza

Turkey
Roll-Ups
with
Chili-Lime
Cream

## Turkey Roll-Ups with Chili-Lime Cream

**8g**
**CARB**

**SERVES** 4
**TOTAL** 15 min.

- ¼ cup light sour cream
- 2 tsp. chili powder
- 1 tsp. lime juice
- 1 low-calorie multigrain flatbread with flax, such as Fit & Active or Flatout
- ¾ cup fresh baby spinach
- ¼ cup bite-size red bell pepper strips
- ¼ cup shredded carrot
- 2 1-oz. slices deli-style lower-sodium turkey breast

**1.** In a bowl stir together sour cream, chili powder, and lime juice. Spread over flatbread. Arrange spinach over sour cream mixture to within 1 inch of one long edge. Sprinkle bell pepper strips and carrot over spinach. Top with turkey slices. Starting from the opposite long edge, tightly roll up flatbread. Cut roll into eight pieces. Serve immediately or cover tightly and refrigerate up to 8 hours before serving. If desired, sprinkle roll-ups with additional chili powder.

**PER SERVING** (2 roll-ups each) **CAL** 68, **FAT** 2 g (1 g sat. fat), **CHOL** 12 mg, **SODIUM** 212 mg, **CARB** 8 g (3 g fiber, 1 g sugars), **PRO** 6 g

# the new veggie chip

Veg out with these snacks. They all make eating more vegetables easy (and tasty!).

## MINI PEPPERS

Start with 3 or 4 mini peppers, halved.

**8 g carb**

2 Tbsp. reduced-fat cream cheese + fresh chives + dash cayenne

**8 g carb**

1 hard-boiled egg, chopped + dash Mrs. Dash original seasoning blend + 2 Tbsp. plain low-fat Greek yogurt

**14 g carb**

¼ cup hummus + 1 Tbsp. low-fat feta cheese + fresh parsley

**12 g carb**

¼ cup low-fat cottage cheese + ¼ cup cherry tomatoes, halved + 1 Tbsp. pine nuts + dash garlic powder

**10 g carb**

½ can albacore white tuna + 2 Tbsp. plain yogurt + 1 Tbsp. lemon juice + 1 Tbsp. finely chopped red onion + lemon zest

# CARROT CHIPS

**Start with ½ cup carrot chips.**

## 18 g carb
3 Tbsp. reduced-sodium black beans + 3 Tbsp. low-sodium salsa + fresh cilantro

## 10 g carb
¼ cup light ricotta + 1 Tbsp. Parmesan cheese + fresh parsley

## 9 g carb
¼ cup plain low-fat Greek yogurt + 1 Tbsp. raisins + 1 Tbsp. finely chopped pistachios

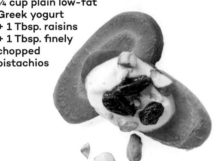

## 14 g carb
¼ cup frozen green peas, thawed + 1 Tbsp. lemon juice + 2 tsp. tahini + fresh mint

## 12 g carb
2 slices lower-sodium, less-fat bacon, cooked and crumbled + 1 tsp. honey

# CUCUMBER SLICES

**Start with ½ cup cucumber slices.**

## 6 g carb
¼ cup low-fat cottage cheese + ¼ cup cherry tomatoes + black pepper

## 5 g carb
¼ cup plain low-fat Greek yogurt + dash garlic powder + 1 tsp. lemon juice + fresh dill + lemon zest

## 11 g carb
3 Tbsp. hummus + 2 Kalamata olives, halved + fresh parsley

## 3 g carb
2 Tbsp. blue cheese crumbles + 1 tsp. finely chopped walnuts

## 6 g carb
¼ cup low-sodium salsa + 1 Tbsp. reduced-fat cheddar cheese + green onion

Sesame-
Almond Bites

Baked Broccoli-Cheddar Quinoa Bites

Carrot Cake Energy Bites

## Sesame-Almond Bites

**7g** CARB

**SERVES** 8
**HANDS ON** 10 min.
**TOTAL** 50 min.

¼ cup sesame seeds
¼ cup unsweetened shredded coconut
¼ cup slivered almonds, toasted
2 Tbsp. honey
1 Tbsp. creamy almond butter
¼ tsp. salt
⅛ tsp. vanilla

**1.** Preheat oven to 325°F. Line a 15×10-inch baking pan with parchment paper. In a bowl stir together all ingredients; mix well. Pat mixture to ¼-inch thickness on the baking pan.
**2.** Bake 13 to 15 minutes or until golden brown. Transfer parchment with mixture to a wire rack and cool completely. Break into ½- to 1-inch pieces.

**PER SERVING** (¼ cup each) **CAL** 83, **FAT** 6 g (2 g sat. fat), **CHOL** 0 mg, **SODIUM** 80 mg, **CARB** 7 g (2 g fiber, 5 g sugars), **PRO** 2 g

## Carrot Cake Energy Bites

**8g** CARB

**SERVES** 22
**HANDS ON** 15 min.
**TOTAL** 15 min.

1 cup pitted dates
½ cup regular rolled oats
¼ cup chopped pecans
¼ cup chia seeds
1 cup finely chopped carrots
1 tsp. vanilla
¾ tsp. ground cinnamon
½ tsp. ground ginger
¼ tsp. ground turmeric
¼ tsp. salt
Pinch black pepper

**1.** In a food processor combine dates, oats, pecans, and chia seeds; pulse until chopped and well combined. Add the remaining ingredients; process until a paste begins to form.
**2.** Roll the mixture into balls using a scant 1 Tbsp. each.

**PER SERVING** (1 bite each) **CAL** 48, **FAT** 2 g (0 g sat. fat), **CHOL** 0 mg, **SODIUM** 30 mg, **CARB** 8 g (2 g fiber, 5 g sugars), **PRO** 1 g

## Baked Broccoli-Cheddar Quinoa Bites

**8g** CARB

**SERVES** 8
**HANDS ON** 20 min.
**TOTAL** 1 hr. 5 min.

Nonstick cooking spray
½ cup dried quinoa
⅛ tsp. + ¼ tsp. salt
¾ cup finely chopped broccoli
¾ cup shredded cheddar cheese (3 oz.)
½ tsp. baking powder
½ tsp. garlic powder
¼ tsp. onion powder
¼ tsp. black pepper
1 large egg, lightly beaten

**1.** Preheat oven to 350°F. Coat 16 cups of a 24-cup mini muffin pan with cooking spray or line with paper bake cups.
**2.** Cook quinoa with ⅛ tsp. of the salt according to package directions.

Remove from heat and let stand, covered, 5 minutes. Transfer to a large bowl and cool at least 10 minutes.
**3.** Add the next six ingredients (through pepper) and the remaining ¼ tsp. salt to the quinoa. Stir in egg.
**4.** Spoon quinoa mixture into the prepared muffin cups; press firmly with lightly moistened fingers. Coat the tops lightly with cooking spray.
**5.** Bake 22 to 25 minutes or until golden. Let cool in pan on a wire rack 20 minutes; remove from pan and cool completely on the wire rack.

**TO STORE** Place bites in an airtight container and store in the refrigerator up to 3 days.

**PER SERVING** (2 bites each) **CAL** 87, **FAT** 4 g (2 g sat. fat), **CHOL** 32 mg, **SODIUM** 209 mg, **CARB** 8 g (1 g fiber, 0 g sugars), **PRO** 5 g

Super-Seed
Squares

## Crunchy Puffed Cherry Granola

**15g CARB**

SERVES 9
HANDS ON 15 min.
TOTAL 30 min.

- 1 cup puffed rice cereal
- 1 cup regular rolled oats
- ½ cup walnuts, coarsely chopped
- 2 Tbsp. unsweetened shredded coconut
- 3 Tbsp. pure maple syrup
- 2 tsp. olive oil
- 1½ tsp. orange zest
- ½ tsp. ground cinnamon
- ¼ tsp. vanilla
- 2 Tbsp. dried tart cherries or dried cranberries, finely chopped

**1.** Preheat oven to 350°F. Line a 15×10-inch baking pan with parchment paper.
**2.** In a bowl stir together rice cereal, oats, walnuts, and coconut. In another bowl whisk together the next five ingredients (through vanilla). Drizzle over oats mixture; stir to coat well. Spread oats mixture in prepared pan.
**3.** Bake about 15 minutes or until golden, stirring after 10 minutes. Remove from oven. Stir in cherries. Let cool on a wire rack.

**TO STORE** Transfer granola to an airtight container. Store at room temperature up to 2 weeks.

**PER SERVING** *(⅓ cup each)* **CAL** 116, **FAT** 6 g *(1 g sat. fat)*, **CHOL** 0 mg, **SODIUM** 2 mg, **CARB** 15 g *(2 g fiber, 6 g sugars)*, **PRO** 2 g

## Super-Seed Squares

**7g CARB**

SERVES 25
HANDS ON 15 min.
TOTAL 1 hr. 10 min.

- Nonstick cooking spray
- ⅓ cup tahini (sesame seed paste)
- ⅓ cup honey
- 1 tsp. vanilla
- ¼ tsp. salt
- 1 cup shredded unsweetened coconut
- ½ cup raw unsalted pumpkin seeds (pepitas)
- ½ cup unsalted sunflower kernels
- ¼ cup chia seeds
- ¼ cup hemp seeds

**1.** Preheat oven to 325°F. Line an 8-inch square pan with parchment paper, extending paper over 2 edges of pan. Coat the parchment paper and pan sides with cooking spray.

**2.** In a small saucepan combine tahini and honey. Cook and stir over medium about 2 minutes or until just mixed and warmed. Remove from heat; stir in vanilla and salt.
**3.** In a large bowl combine the remaining ingredients. Add the tahini mixture; stir until evenly coated. Press the mixture firmly into the prepared pan.
**4.** Bake 30 to 35 minutes or until golden. Cool completely in pan on a wire rack. Use parchment to lift uncut squares out of pan; cut into 25 squares.

**TO STORE** Place squares in an airtight container. Store in the refrigerator up to 1 week.

**PER SERVING** *(1 square each)* **CAL** 110, **FAT** 9 g *(3 g sat. fat)*, **CHOL** 0 mg, **SODIUM** 27 mg, **CARB** 7 g *(2 g fiber, 4 g sugars)*, **PRO** 3 g

Crunchy
Puffed
Cherry
Granola

# 8

# DELIGHTFUL
# DESSERTS

When you crave sweet, look to this chapter
for dessert makeovers with carb profiles that
fit your meal plan with 200 calories or less.
These sensibly sweet recipes include
reduced-sugar Dessert Pizza with Banana
Nice Cream and kid-friendly, make-ahead
Creamy Chocolate Pie Ice Pops.

143

147

153

Blueberry
Lemon Curd
Ice Cream
Cake

## Blueberry Lemon Curd Ice Cream Cake

**30g**
**CARB**

**SERVES** 20
**HANDS ON** 20 min.
**TOTAL** 1 hr. + overnight freezing

Nonstick cooking spray
1 16-oz. box sugar-free yellow cake mix
1 cup water
3 eggs
¼ cup canola oil
1 Tbsp. lemon zest
½ of a 10-oz. jar lemon curd
4 cups no-sugar-added vanilla ice cream, slightly softened
1 cup assorted fresh berries

1. Preheat oven to 325°F. Lightly coat a 10-inch springform pan with cooking spray; line with parchment paper. In a large bowl combine the next five ingredients (through lemon zest). Beat with a mixer on medium 2 minutes. Pour batter into the prepared pan.
2. Bake 35 to 38 minutes or until a toothpick inserted in center comes out clean. Cool in pan on a wire rack.
3. Spread lemon curd over top of cake; spoon ice cream over lemon curd, smoothing top. Cover and freeze overnight.
4. Remove cake from freezer; let stand 5 minutes before removing sides of pan. Top with berries.

**PER SERVING** *(1 slice each)* **CAL** 171, **FAT** 8 g *(2 g sat. fat)*, **CHOL** 38 mg, **SODIUM** 206 mg, **CARB** 30 g *(2 g fiber, 7 g sugars)*, **PRO** 3 g

Lemon-Berry Pudding Cake

## Lemon-Berry Pudding Cake

**29g**
**CARB**

**SERVES** 6
**HANDS ON** 20 min.
**SLOW COOK** 2 hr. 30 min.

3 eggs
Nonstick cooking spray
1 cup fresh blueberries and/or fresh red raspberries
1 Tbsp. granulated sugar
½ cup granulated sugar
¼ cup all-purpose flour
2 tsp. lemon zest
¼ tsp. salt
1 cup fat-free milk
3 Tbsp. lemon juice
3 Tbsp. tub-style vegetable oil spread
Powdered sugar (optional)

1. Let eggs stand at room temperature 30 minutes. Meanwhile, coat a 2-qt. slow cooker with cooking spray. Place berries in cooker and sprinkle with the 1 Tbsp. granulated sugar.
2. For batter, separate eggs. In a medium bowl combine the ½ cup granulated sugar, the flour, lemon zest, and salt. Add milk, lemon juice, vegetable oil spread, and egg yolks. Beat with a mixer on low until combined. Beat on medium 1 minute.
3. Thoroughly wash beaters. In another bowl beat egg whites with mixer on medium until soft peaks form (tips curl). Fold egg whites into batter. Carefully pour batter over berries in cooker, spreading evenly.
4. Cover and cook on high 2½ to 3 hours. (If possible, rotate the crockery liner 180° halfway through cooking for even browning.) Turn off cooker. If possible, remove crockery liner from cooker. Cool, uncovered, on a wire rack 1 hour before serving. If desired, sprinkle with powdered sugar.

**PER SERVING** *(⅔ cup each)* **CAL** 200, **FAT** 7 g *(2 g sat. fat)*, **CHOL** 94 mg, **SODIUM** 188 mg, **CARB** 29 g *(1 g fiber, 24 g sugars)*, **PRO** 5 g

Summer
Berry Bread
Pudding
with Mint
Gremolata

## Summer Berry Bread Pudding with Mint Gremolata

**25g CARB**

| | |
|---|---|
| **SERVES** 12 | |
| **HANDS ON** 30 min. | |
| **TOTAL** 1 hr. 30 min. | |

- 10 oz. multigrain bread, cut into ½-inch cubes (8 cups)
- 2 cups fresh blackberries
- 1¼ cups sliced fresh strawberries
- 1 cup fresh blueberries
- 1 cup fresh raspberries
- 1 cup apple juice
- ¼ cup sugar
- ¼ tsp. salt
- 2 tsp. vanilla
- ¼ cup broken pecans, toasted and chopped
- 2 Tbsp. finely chopped fresh mint or basil leaves
- 1 Tbsp. orange zest
- ¾ cup frozen light whipped dessert topping, thawed

**1.** Preheat oven to 300°F. Arrange bread cubes in a single layer in a shallow baking pan. Bake 10 to 15 minutes or until very dry, stirring once or twice. Cool completely. (Cubes will continue to dry as they cool.)
**2.** Meanwhile, in a 3-qt. saucepan combine the next seven ingredients (through salt). Cook over medium about 5 minutes or until sugar is dissolved and mixture is heated through, stirring gently to break up some of the berries. (Most of the berries should remain intact.) Remove from heat. Stir in vanilla. Cool completely.
**3.** Arrange one-third of the bread cubes in the bottom of a large clear-glass bowl. Top with 2 cups of the berry mixture. Repeat layers twice. Using the back of a large spoon, press down on layers. Cover and chill 1 hour.
**4.** For gremolata, in a small bowl combine pecans, mint, and orange zest. Top servings with dessert topping and sprinkle with gremolata.

**PER SERVING** (⅔ cup each) **CAL** 145, **FAT** 3 g (1 g sat. fat), **CHOL** 0 mg, **SODIUM** 151 mg, **CARB** 25 g (5 g fiber, 12 g sugars), **PRO** 4 g

Strawberry Cream Pie

## Strawberry Cream Pie

**22g CARB**

| | |
|---|---|
| **SERVES** 8 | |
| **HANDS ON** 30 min. | |
| **TOTAL** 4 hr. 30 min. | |

- 2½ cups fresh strawberries
- ¼ cup sugar
- 1 envelope unflavored gelatin
- 2 Tbsp. frozen limeade concentrate or frozen lemonade concentrate, thawed
- 3 egg whites, slightly beaten
- 1 Tbsp. tequila or orange juice
- 1 3-oz. pkg. ladyfingers, split
- 2 Tbsp. orange juice
- ½ of an 8-oz. container frozen light whipped dessert topping, thawed
  Sliced fresh strawberries (optional)
  Fresh mint (optional)

**1.** Place the 2½ cups strawberries in a blender or food processor. Cover and blend until nearly smooth. Measure strawberries (you should have about 1½ cups.)
**2.** In a medium saucepan stir together the sugar and gelatin. Stir in the blended strawberries and limeade concentrate. Cook and stir over medium until mixture bubbles and gelatin is dissolved. Gradually stir about half of the strawberry mixture into the egg whites. Return mixture to the saucepan. Cook over low about 3 minutes or until mixture is slightly thickened, stirring constantly. Do not boil. Pour into a medium bowl; stir in tequila. Chill about 2 hours or until mixture mounds when spooned, stirring occasionally.
**3.** Meanwhile, cut half of the split ladyfingers in half crosswise; stand on end around the outside edge of a 9-inch tart pan with a removable bottom or a 9-inch springform pan. Arrange the remaining split ladyfingers in the bottom of the pan. Drizzle the 2 Tbsp. orange juice over the ladyfingers.
**4.** Fold whipped topping into strawberry mixture. Spoon into the prepared pan. Cover and chill about 2 hours or until set. If desired, garnish with sliced strawberries and mint.

**PER SERVING** (1 wedge each) **CAL** 130, **FAT** 3 g (2 g sat. fat), **CHOL** 39 mg, **SODIUM** 48 mg, **CARB** 22 g (1 g fiber, 0 g sugars), **PRO** 4 g

# dessert toppers

Dish up ½ cup half-the-fat vanilla or chocolate ice cream. Make it yours with smart portions of tasty toppers.

## S'MORES TOPPER

Drizzle **1 Tbsp. sugar-free chocolate-flavor syrup** over ice cream. Top with about **12 tiny marshmallows** and **¼ of a large graham cracker rectangle, coarsely crushed.**

**SERVES 1. CAL** 132, **CARB** 24 g *(0 g fiber, 13 g sugars)*

## PB&J TOPPER

In a small bowl mash **¼ cup chopped fresh strawberries** with a fork; spoon over ice cream. Melt **1 tsp. creamy peanut butter** with **2 tsp. fat-free milk.** Stir together until smooth; drizzle over ice cream. Top with **2 Tbsp. chopped fresh strawberries.**

**SERVES 1. CAL** 153, **CARB** 23 g *(1 g fiber, 15 g sugars)*

## MINT CHOCOLATE CHIP TOPPER

Melt **2 tsp. dark chocolate chips.** Drizzle over ice cream. Top with **1 chopped layered chocolate-mint candy, such as Andes,** and **fresh mint leaves.**

**SERVES 1. CAL** 172, **CARB** 26 g *(1 g fiber, 19 g sugars)*

## CHERRY-BERRY TOPPER

Cook **¼ cup frozen unsweetened tart red cherries** and **2 Tbsp. water** in a small saucepan over medium until slightly thickened, stirring to break up cherries. Spoon over ice cream. Top with **2 Tbsp. fresh blackberries** and **1 Tbsp. chopped dry-roasted pistachio nuts.**

**SERVES 1. CAL** 171, **CARB** 25 g *(2 g fiber, 16 g sugars)*

## TRIPLE CITRUS TOPPER

In a small saucepan simmer **¼ cup orange juice** and **¼ cup refrigerated unsweetened coconut milk beverage** over medium until reduced to 2 Tbsp. Stir in **¼ tsp. lime zest.** Drizzle over ice cream. Top with **1 Tbsp. unsweetened coconut flakes, toasted,** and **¼ tsp. lemon zest.** Serve with a **lime wedge.**

**SERVES 1. CAL** 167, **CARB** 25 g *(1 g fiber, 17 g sugars)*

## APPLE-CARAMEL TOPPER

Drizzle ice cream with **1 Tbsp. sugar-free caramel ice cream topping.** Top with **¼ cup chopped apple, 1 Tbsp. low-fat granola,** and a **dash of apple pie spice or ground cinnamon.**

**SERVES 1. CAL** 153, **CARB** 30 g *(1 g fiber, 16 g sugars)*

## MAPLE PECAN TOPPER

Toast **1 Tbsp. chopped pecans** and toss with a **dash of pumpkin pie spice or apple pie spice.** Top ice cream with pecans and **1 tsp. pure maple syrup.** Sprinkle with additional **pumpkin pie spice or apple pie spice.**

**SERVES 1. CAL** 165, **CARB** 23 g *(1 g fiber, 15 g sugars)*

Chocolate
Peanut
Butter Swirl
Snack Cake

Dessert
Pizza with
Banana Nice
Cream

## Chocolate Peanut Butter Swirl Snack Cake

**12g**
**CARB**

| | |
|---|---|
| **SERVES** 32 | |
| **HANDS ON** 20 min. | |
| **TOTAL** 50 min. | |

1 cup plain fat-free Greek yogurt
1 cup water
1 16-oz. pkg. sugar-free devil's food cake mix
⅓ cup creamy peanut butter
¼ cup fat-free milk
2 Tbsp. plain fat-free Greek yogurt
¼ cup refrigerated or frozen egg product, thawed, or 1 egg, lightly beaten

**1.** Preheat oven to 350°F. Grease and flour two 8×4-inch loaf pans. In a bowl whisk together the 1 cup yogurt and the water. Add cake mix; stir just until smooth (batter will be thick).
**2.** In another bowl whisk together peanut butter, milk, and the 2 Tbsp. yogurt until smooth. Whisk in egg. Add ¼ cup of the chocolate batter to peanut butter mixture; whisk just until combined.
**3.** Spoon half of the remaining chocolate batter into the prepared loaf pans, spreading evenly. Drizzle half of the peanut butter mixture over batter in pans. Repeat layers. Using a thin metal spatula, swirl mixtures together.
**4.** Bake about 30 minutes or until a toothpick inserted in centers comes out clean. Cool 10 minutes in pans on a wire rack. Remove from pans; cool completely on wire rack.

**TO STORE** Wrap loaves in plastic wrap and place in a resealable plastic bag. Store at room temperature up to 3 days or freeze up to 1 month.

**PER SERVING** (1 slice each) **CAL** 64, **FAT** 2 g (0 g sat. fat), **CHOL** 0 mg, **SODIUM** 117 mg, **CARB** 12 g (1 g fiber, 1 g sugars), **PRO** 2 g

**TIP**
It's best to use the bananas directly from the freezer without letting them thaw.

## Dessert Pizza with Banana Nice Cream

**17g CARB**

SERVES 12
HANDS ON 20 min.
TOTAL 45 min.

- 2 cups crisp rice cereal
- 1 Tbsp. unsweetened cocoa powder
- 2 Tbsp. coconut oil, melted
- 2 Tbsp. honey
- 1 recipe Banana Nice Cream Topper(s), such as berries, sliced fruit, and/or chopped nuts

**1.** For crust, line a 12-inch pizza pan with parchment paper. In a medium bowl stir together cereal and cocoa powder. Stir in oil and honey. Spread into a 10-inch circle in prepared pan. Freeze 5 to 10 minutes or until firm.
**2.** If necessary, let Banana Nice Cream stand at room temperature just until soft enough to spread. Spread over crust to within 1 inch of the edges; add topper(s). Freeze 20 to 30 minutes or until ice cream is nearly firm.

**PER SERVING** *(1 wedge each)* **CAL** 111,
**FAT** 4 g *(2 g sat. fat)*, **CHOL** 0 mg, **SODIUM** 27 mg,
**CARB** 17 g *(2 g fiber, 9 g sugars)*, **PRO** 2 g

## Banana Nice Cream

**18g CARB**

SERVES 6
TOTAL 10 min.

- 4 medium bananas, peeled, sliced, and frozen
- ¼ cup refrigerated unsweetened coconut milk
- 2 teaspoons vanilla

**1.** In a food processor combine all ingredients. Cover; process until smooth. Serve immediately for soft-serve ice cream or freeze at least 4 hours for scoopable ice cream. Store in freezer up to 1 week.

**PER SERVING** *(½ cup each)* **CAL** 76, **FAT** 0 g,
**CHOL** 0 mg, **SODIUM** 3 mg, **CARB** 18 g *(2 g fiber,
10 g sugars)*, **PRO** 1 g,

**CHOCOLATE NICE CREAM** Prepare as directed, except add 2 Tbsp. unsweetened cocoa powder and reduce coconut milk to 2 Tbsp.

**PER SERVING** *(½ cup each)* **CAL** 79,
**FAT** 1 g *(0 g sat. fat)*, **CHOL** 0 mg, **SODIUM** 3 mg,
**CARB** 19 g *(3 g fiber, 10 g sugars)*, **PRO** 1 g,

### Raspberry Clafouti

**18g CARB**

SERVES 8
HANDS ON 20 min.
TOTAL 1 hr. 25 min.

Nonstick cooking spray
1 vanilla bean, split lengthwise
1 cup low-fat (1%) milk
3 eggs
½ cup white whole wheat flour
¼ cup granulated sugar
2 Tbsp. butter, melted
¼ tsp. almond extract
⅛ tsp. salt
2 cups fresh raspberries
1 tsp. powdered sugar

**1.** Preheat oven to 350°F. Coat a 9-inch pie plate with cooking spray.

**2.** Using the tip of a sharp knife, scrape seeds from vanilla bean. Place seeds in a small saucepan; add milk and the vanilla bean pod. Bring to simmering over medium; remove from heat. Let stand 15 minutes; discard pod.

**3.** For batter, in a blender combine the next six ingredients (through salt). Add milk mixture. Cover and blend until smooth. Arrange raspberries in the prepared pie plate. Pour batter over raspberries.

**4.** Bake about 35 minutes or until puffed and edges are light brown. Cool on a wire rack 15 minutes. Dust with powdered sugar and, if desired, top with additional raspberries. Serve warm.

**PER SERVING** (1 slice each) **CAL** 135, **FAT** 5 g (3 g sat. fat), **CHOL** 79 mg, **SODIUM** 100 mg, **CARB** 18 g (3 g fiber, 10 g sugars), **PRO** 5 g

Raspberry-
Lemon
Chiffon Ice
Box Cake

## Raspberry-Lemon Chiffon Ice Box Cake

**21g**
CARB

**SERVES** 10
**HANDS ON** 35 min.
**TOTAL** 2 hr. 35 min.

Nonstick cooking spray
4 cups fresh raspberries
½ cup water
1 Tbsp. sugar
1¼ tsp. unflavored gelatin
1 8-oz. container frozen light whipped dessert topping, thawed
½ of a 4-serving-size pkg. fat-free, sugar-free, reduced-calorie lemon instant pudding mix
½ cup fat-free milk
8 2½-inch squares graham crackers, finely crushed
2 Tbsp. butter, melted
Fresh mint leaves (optional)

**1.** Coat an 8×4-inch loaf pan with cooking spray. Line pan with a double layer of plastic wrap, extending wrap 2 inches over sides.
**2.** In a large saucepan combine raspberries and ¼ cup of the water; mash berries. Bring to boiling; reduce heat. Simmer, uncovered, 10 minutes. Press through a fine-mesh sieve; discard seeds. Return puree to saucepan; stir in sugar. Simmer, uncovered, about 10 minutes more or until reduced to ½ cup. Cool slightly.
**3.** In a small saucepan sprinkle gelatin over the remaining ¼ cup water; do not stir. Let stand 5 minutes. Heat and stir over medium just until gelatin is dissolved. Stir gelatin mixture into berry mixture. Stir in ½ cup of the whipped topping until combined. Fold in another ½ cup of the whipped topping until no streaks remain. Spoon into the prepared loaf pan. Cover and chill 1 hour or just until set.
**4.** In a medium bowl whisk together pudding mix and milk until thick. Whisk in one-third of the remaining whipped topping until combined. Fold in the remaining whipped topping until no streaks remain. Spread over raspberry layer.
**5.** In a small bowl combine graham crackers and melted butter. Gently press mixture onto pudding layer. Cover and chill 1 to 8 hours.
**6.** Using plastic wrap, lift out cake. Invert onto a serving plate and, if desired, top with additional raspberries and mint.

Orange Flan

**PER SERVING** *(1 slice each)* **CAL** 138, **FAT** 6 g *(4 g sat. fat)*, **CHOL** 6 mg, **SODIUM** 109 mg, **CARB** 21 g *(3 g fiber, 8 g sugars)*, **PRO** 2 g

## Orange Flan

**23g**
CARB

**SERVES** 8
**HANDS ON** 20 min.
**TOTAL** 5 hr. 45 min.

¾ cup sugar
2 oranges
4 eggs
1 cup fat-free milk
⅔ cup half-and-half
¼ cup sugar
⅛ tsp. salt
Sliced kumquats and/or edible flowers (optional)

**1.** Preheat oven to 325°F. Place a 9-inch pie plate in a large roasting pan. In a heavy large skillet heat ½ cup of the sugar over medium-high until sugar begins to melt, shaking skillet occasionally for even melting. Do not stir. When sugar starts to melt, reduce heat to low; cook about 5 minutes or until all of the sugar is melted and golden, stirring with a wooden spoon. Immediately pour melted sugar into pie plate; tilt the pie plate to spread the melted sugar (sugar will harden quickly in the pie plate).
**2.** Remove ½ tsp. zest and squeeze ⅓ cup juice from oranges. In a large bowl whisk together orange zest and juice, eggs, milk, half-and-half, the remaining ¼ cup sugar, and the salt. Pour mixture into pie plate. Place roasting pan on oven rack. Pour enough boiling water into roasting pan around pie plate to come halfway up the sides of the pie plate.
**3.** Bake about 55 minutes or until a knife inserted near the center comes out clean. Carefully remove pie plate from water. Cool on a wire rack 30 minutes. Cover and chill 4 to 24 hours.
**4.** To serve, invert flan onto a platter. If desired, top with kumquats and/or edible flowers.

**PER SERVING** *(⅓ wedge each)* **CAL** 149, **FAT** 5 g *(2 g sat. fat)*, **CHOL** 101 mg, **SODIUM** 97 mg, **CARB** 23 g *(0 g fiber, 22 g sugars)*, **PRO** 5 g

## Blueberry-Swirl Buttermilk Ice Cream

**19g CARB**

**SERVES** 12
**HANDS ON** 20 min.
**TOTAL** 15 hr.

- 2 eggs
- ¾ cup sugar
- ¼ tsp. salt
- 1 cup buttermilk
- 2 cups plain whole milk Greek yogurt
- 1 12-oz. pkg. frozen unsweetened blueberries
- 2 Tbsp. lemon juice
  Fresh blueberries (optional)
  Fresh mint (optional)

**1.** In a medium heavy saucepan whisk together eggs, ½ cup of the sugar, and the salt until slightly thick; whisk in buttermilk. Cook and stir over medium-low about 10 minutes or until mixture coats the back of a metal spoon (165°F). Set saucepan in a large bowl of ice water and stir mixture until cooled. Stir in yogurt. Cover and chill 8 to 24 hours.

**2.** Meanwhile, in a small saucepan combine frozen blueberries, the remaining ¼ cup sugar, and the lemon juice. Bring to boiling over medium-high, whisking frequently; reduce heat.

Simmer, uncovered, about 5 minutes or until syrupy; cool. Transfer to a bowl. Cover and chill 8 to 24 hours.

**3.** Freeze chilled buttermilk mixture in a 1½- or 2-qt. ice cream freezer according to manufacturer's directions. Transfer to a freezer container. Swirl blueberry mixture into ice cream. Cover and freeze 6 to 8 hours or until firm. Let stand at room temperature 20 to 30 minutes before serving. If desired, top servings with fresh blueberries and mint.

**PER SERVING** *(½ cup each)* **CAL** 122, **FAT** 3 g *(2 g sat. fat)*, **CHOL** 37 mg, **SODIUM** 95 mg, **CARB** 19 g *(1 g fiber, 18 g sugars)*, **PRO** 5 g

**TO TOTE**

Seal jars and tote in an insulated bag or cooler with an ice pack.

### Key Lime Mason Jar Cheesecakes

**16g**
**CARB**

**SERVES** 8
**TOTAL** 20 min.

- ⅔ cup crushed graham crackers
- 1 Tbsp. butter, melted
- 2 oz. reduced-fat cream cheese (neufchatel), softened
- 2 Tbsp. Key lime juice
- ¼ tsp. vanilla
- ¼ cup powdered sugar

- 2 cups frozen light whipped topping, thawed
  Thin Key lime slices

1. In a small bowl stir together crushed graham crackers and melted butter. Divide mixture among eight 4-oz. canning jars; press lightly with the back of a spoon.

2. For filling, in a large bowl beat cream cheese with a mixer on medium 30 seconds. Beat in lime juice and vanilla. Beat in powdered sugar until smooth. Fold in about ½ cup of the whipped topping to lighten. Fold in the remaining whipped topping. Transfer to a heavy resealable plastic bag; snip a 1-inch hole in a corner of the bag. Pipe filling into jars. Top with lime slices. Serve immediately or cover and chill up to 24 hours.

**PER SERVING** (⅓ cup each) **CAL** 118, **FAT** 6 g (4 g sat. fat), **CHOL** 9 mg, **SODIUM** 67 mg, **CARB** 16 g (0 g fiber, 8 g sugars), **PRO** 1 g

Mango
Tiramisu

## Mango Tiramisu

**27g**
**CARB**

SERVES 8
HANDS ON 30 min.
TOTAL 8 hr. 30 min.

- 2 **medium mangoes, halved, seeded, peeled, and cubed**
- 2 **Tbsp. light agave syrup**
- ¼ **tsp. almond extract**
- 1 **cup frozen light whipped topping, thawed**
- 1 **cup vanilla fat-free Greek yogurt**
- 12 **crisp ladyfingers, broken into 1-inch pieces**

**1.** Place half of the mango cubes in a food processor; cover and process until smooth. Transfer mango puree to a small bowl. Stir in agave syrup and almond extract. Add the remaining mango cubes to food processor; cover and pulse until coarsely chopped.

**2.** In another small bowl gently fold whipped topping into yogurt.
**3.** Sprinkle half of the ladyfinger pieces into a 2-qt. shallow baking dish. Spoon half of the mango puree and yogurt mixture over ladyfingers in dish. Top with chopped mango. Repeat layering the remaining ladyfingers, mango puree, and yogurt mixture in dish.
**4.** Cover with plastic wrap and chill 8 to 24 hours or until ladyfingers are softened. If desired, top servings with additional mango. Serve cold.

**TIP** If you can't find fresh mangoes, use 16 oz. frozen chopped mango, thawed, or refrigerated mango slices.

**PER SERVING** (⅔ cup each) **CAL** 147, **FAT** 3 g (2 g sat. fat), **CHOL** 37 mg, **SODIUM** 35 mg, **CARB** 27 g (1 g fiber, 14 g sugars), **PRO** 5 g

## Classic Cherry Crisp

**30g**
**CARB**

SERVES 6
TOTAL 25 min.

- 1 **orange**
- ½ **cup regular rolled oats**
- ¼ **cup almond flour**
- ¼ **cup packed brown sugar**
- 2 **Tbsp. unsalted butter, melted**
- 2 **Tbsp. sliced almonds**
- 2 **Tbsp. flaxseed meal**
- 1 **tsp. ground cinnamon**
- 1 **lb. fresh or frozen unsweetened pitted dark sweet or tart red cherries**
- 1 **Tbsp. cornstarch**
  **Vanilla low-fat frozen yogurt (optional)**

**1.** Remove 1 tsp. zest and squeeze ¼ cup juice from orange.
**2.** For topping, heat a medium cast-iron or heavy skillet over medium. Add oats; cook about 3 minutes or until toasted, stirring occasionally. Add the next six ingredients (through cinnamon). Cook and stir about 1 minute or until mixture clings together in coarse crumbs (watch carefully; topping can brown quickly). Remove from skillet.
**3.** In the same skillet combine cherries and cornstarch; stir in orange zest and juice. Cook and stir over medium-high until thick and bubbly. Cook and stir 2 minutes more.
**4.** Sprinkle cherry mixture with topping. If desired, serve with vanilla frozen yogurt.

**PER SERVING** (½ cup each) **CAL** 203, **FAT** 9 g (3 g sat. fat), **CHOL** 10 mg, **SODIUM** 6 mg, **CARB** 30 g (4 g fiber, 20 g sugars), **PRO** 4 g

Classic
Cherry Crisp

Pineapple,
Kiwi, and
Honeydew
Ice Pops

## Pineapple, Kiwi, and Honeydew Ice Pops

**18g** CARB

**SERVES** 8
**HANDS ON** 25 min.
**TOTAL** 8 hr. 25 min.

¼ cup water
2 Tbsp. sugar
2 cups cubed fresh pineapple
2 fresh kiwifruit, peeled and cut into 16 slices
3½ cups cubed honeydew melon

**1.** In a small bowl combine the water and sugar, stirring until sugar is dissolved. In a blender or food processor combine pineapple and 1 Tbsp. of the sugar mixture. Cover and blend or process until smooth.
**2.** Pour mixture into eight 5-oz. paper cups or ice-pop molds. Press two kiwi slices down opposite sides of each cup. Freeze about 2 hours or until thick and slushy.
**3.** In blender or food processor combine honeydew and the remaining sugar mixture. Cover and blend or process until smooth. Pour over pineapple layer. Cover each cup with foil; cut a small slit in foil and insert a wooden stick into each pop. Or insert sticks into molds. Freeze overnight or until firm.

**PER SERVING** *(1 ice pop each)* **CAL** 71, **FAT** 0 g, **CHOL** 0 mg, **SODIUM** 15 mg, **CARB** 18 g *(2 g fiber, 15 g sugars)*, **PRO** 1 g

Creamy Chocolate Pie Ice Pops

## Creamy Chocolate Pie Ice Pops

**9g** CARB

**SERVES** 9
**HANDS ON** 15 min.
**TOTAL** 8 hr. 15 min.

1 4-serving-size pkg. fat-free, sugar-free, reduced-calorie chocolate instant pudding mix
2 cups unsweetened almond milk or fat-free milk
1 cup frozen light whipped topping, thawed
1 oz. dark chocolate, melted
1 Tbsp. crushed graham crackers

**1.** In a medium bowl whisk together pudding mix and almond milk; continue whisking 2 to 3 minutes or until thick. Fold in whipped topping.
**2.** Spoon mixture into nine 3-oz. paper cups or ice pop molds. Insert sticks in molds. If using paper cups, cover each cup with foil. Cut small slits in foil and insert a wooden stick into each pop. Freeze overnight or until firm.
**3.** Unmold pops. Working with one pop at a time, drizzle with melted chocolate and immediately sprinkle with graham crackers.

**PER SERVING** *(1 ice pop each)* **CAL** 60, **FAT** 3 g *(2 g sat. fat)*, **CHOL** 0 mg, **SODIUM** 175 mg, **CARB** 9 g *(1 g fiber, 2 g sugars)*, **PRO** 1 g

# RECIPE GUIDE

## Inside Our Recipes

Precise serving sizes (listed with nutrition facts) help you to manage portions.

Test Kitchen tips are listed after the recipe directions.

When kitchen basics such as ice, salt, black pepper, and nonstick cooking spray are not listed in the ingredients list, they are italicized in the directions.

### Ingredients

* Tub-style vegetable oil spread refers to 60% to 70% vegetable oil product.
* Lean ground beef refers to 95% or leaner ground beef.

## Nutrition Information

Nutrition facts per serving are noted with each recipe.

Ingredients listed as optional are not included in the per-serving nutrition analysis.

When ingredient choices appear, we use the first one to calculate the nutrition analysis.

### Key to Abbreviations

CAL = calories
sat. fat = saturated fat
CHOL = cholesterol
CARB = carbohydrate
PRO = protein

## Handling Hot Chile Peppers

Chile peppers can irritate skin and eyes. Wear gloves when working with them. If your bare hands do touch the peppers, wash your hands with soap and warm water.

# RECIPE INDEX

# METRIC INFORMATION

The charts on this page provide a guide for converting measurements from the U.S. customary system, which is used throughout this book, to the metric system.

## Product Differences

Most of the ingredients called for in the recipes in this book are available in most countries. However, some are known by different names. Here are some common American ingredients and their possible counterparts:

* All-purpose flour is enriched, bleached or unbleached white household flour. When self-rising flour is used in place of all-purpose flour in a recipe that calls for leavening, omit the leavening agent (baking soda or baking powder) and salt.
* Baking soda is bicarbonate of soda.
* Cornstarch is cornflour.
* Golden raisins are sultanas.
* Light-color corn syrup is golden syrup.
* Powdered sugar is icing sugar.
* Sugar (white) is granulated, fine granulated, or castor sugar.
* Vanilla or vanilla extract is vanilla essence.

## Volume and Weight

The United States traditionally uses cup measures for liquid and solid ingredients. The chart below shows the approximate imperial and metric equivalents. If you are accustomed to weighing solid ingredients, the following approximate equivalents will be helpful.

* 1 cup butter, castor sugar, or rice = 8 ounces = $\frac{1}{2}$ pound = 250 grams
* 1 cup flour = 4 ounces = $\frac{1}{4}$ pound = 125 grams
* 1 cup icing sugar = 5 ounces = 150 grams

Canadian and U.S. volume for a cup measure is 8 fluid ounces (237 ml), but the standard metric equivalent is 250 ml.

1 British imperial cup is 10 fluid ounces.

In Australia, 1 tablespoon equals 20 ml, and there are 4 teaspoons in the Australian tablespoon.

Spoon measures are used for smaller amounts of ingredients. Although the size of the tablespoon varies slightly in different countries, for practical purposes and for recipes in this book, a straight substitution is all that's necessary. Measurements made using cups or spoons always should be level unless stated otherwise.

## Common Weight Range Replacements

| Imperial/U.S. | Metric |
|---|---|
| $\frac{1}{2}$ ounce | 15 g |
| 1 ounce | 25 g or 30 g |
| 4 ounces ($\frac{1}{4}$ pound) | 115 g or 125 g |
| 8 ounces ($\frac{1}{2}$ pound) | 225 g or 250 g |
| 16 ounces (1 pound) | 450 g or 500 g |
| $1\frac{1}{4}$ pounds | 625 g |
| $1\frac{1}{2}$ pounds | 750 g |
| 2 pounds or $2\frac{1}{4}$ pounds | 1,000 g or 1 Kg |

## Oven Temperature Equivalents

| Fahrenheit Setting | Celsius Setting* | Gas Setting |
|---|---|---|
| 300°F | 150°C | Gas Mark 2 (very low) |
| 325°F | 160°C | Gas Mark 3 (low) |
| 350°F | 180°C | Gas Mark 4 (moderate) |
| 375°F | 190°C | Gas Mark 5 (moderate) |
| 400°F | 200°C | Gas Mark 6 (hot) |
| 425°F | 220°C | Gas Mark 7 (hot) |
| 450°F | 230°C | Gas Mark 8 (very hot) |
| 475°F | 240°C | Gas Mark 9 (very hot) |
| 500°F | 260°C | Gas Mark 10 (extremely hot) |
| Broil | Broil | Grill |

*Electric and gas ovens may be calibrated using celsius. However, for an electric oven, increase celsius setting 10 to 20 degrees when cooking above 160°C. For convection or forced air ovens (gas or electric), lower the temperature setting 25°F/10°C when cooking at all heat levels.*

## Baking Pan Sizes

| Imperial/U.S. | Metric |
|---|---|
| 9×1$\frac{1}{2}$-inch round cake pan | 22- or 23×4-cm (1.5 L) |
| 9×1$\frac{1}{2}$-inch pie plate | 22- or 23×4-cm (1 L) |
| 8×8×2-inch square cake pan | 20×5-cm (2 L) |
| 9×9×2-inch square cake pan | 22- or 23×4.5-cm (2.5 L) |
| 11×7×1$\frac{1}{2}$-inch baking pan | 28×17×4-cm (2 L) |
| 2-quart rectangular baking pan | 30×19×4.5-cm (3 L) |
| 13×9×2-inch baking pan | 34×22×4.5-cm (3.5 L) |
| 15×10×1-inch jelly roll pan | 40×25×2-cm |
| 9×5×3-inch loaf pan | 23×13×8-cm (2 L) |
| 2-quart casserole | 2 L |

## U.S. / Standard Metric Equivalents

| | |
|---|---|
| $\frac{1}{8}$ teaspoon = 0.5 ml | |
| $\frac{1}{4}$ teaspoon = 1 ml | |
| $\frac{1}{2}$ teaspoon = 2 ml | |
| 1 teaspoon = 5 ml | |
| 1 tablespoon = 15 ml | |
| 2 tablespoons = 25 ml | |
| $\frac{1}{4}$ cup = 2 fluid ounces = 50 ml | |
| $\frac{1}{3}$ cup = 3 fluid ounces = 75 ml | |
| $\frac{1}{2}$ cup = 4 fluid ounces = 125 ml | |
| $\frac{2}{3}$ cup = 5 fluid ounces = 150 ml | |
| $\frac{3}{4}$ cup = 6 fluid ounces = 175 ml | |
| 1 cup = 8 fluid ounces = 250 ml | |
| 2 cups = 1 pint = 500 ml | |
| 1 quart = 1 litre | |